Thomas Nelson Page

The Burial of the Guns

Thomas Nelson Page

The Burial of the Guns

ISBN/EAN: 9783337011611

Printed in Europe, USA, Canada, Australia, Japan

Cover: Foto ©ninafisch / pixelio.de

More available books at **www.hansebooks.com**

THE
BURIAL OF THE GUNS

BY

THOMAS NELSON PAGE

NEW YORK
CHARLES SCRIBNER'S SONS
1894

COPYRIGHT, 1894, BY
CHARLES SCRIBNER'S SONS

TROW DIRECTORY
PRINTING AND BOOKBINDING COMPANY
NEW YORK

TO MY WIFE

CONTENTS

	PAGE
MY COUSIN FANNY	1
THE BURIAL OF THE GUNS	41
THE GRAY JACKET OF "NO. 4"	87
MISS DANGERLIE'S ROSES	119
HOW THE CAPTAIN MADE CHRISTMAS	145
LITTLE DARBY	173

My Cousin Fanny

MY COUSIN FANNY

WE do not keep Christmas now as we used to do in old Hanover. We have not time for it, and it does not seem like the same thing. Christmas, however, always brings up to me my cousin Fanny; I suppose because she always was so foolish about Christmas.

My cousin Fanny was an old maid; indeed, to follow St. Paul's turn of phrase, she was an old maid of the old maids. No one who saw her a moment could have doubted it. Old maids have from most people a feeling rather akin to pity—a hard heritage. They very often have this feeling from the young. This must be the hardest part of all—to see around them friends, each "a happy mother of children," little ones responding to affection with the sweet caresses of childhood, whilst any advances that they, their aunts or cousins, may make are met with indifference or condescension. My cousin Fanny was no exception. She was as proud as Lucifer; yet she went through life—the part that I knew of—bearing the pity of the great majority of the people who knew her.

She lived at an old place called "Woodside," which had been in the family for a great many years; indeed, ever since before the Revolution. The neighborhood dated back to the time of the colony, and Woodside was one of the old places. My cousin Fanny's grandmother had stood in the door of her chamber with her large scissors in her hand, and defied Tarleton's red-coated troopers to touch the basket of old communion-plate which she had hung on her arm.

The house was a large brick edifice, with a pyramidal roof, covered with moss, small windows, porticos with pillars somewhat out of repair, a big, high hall, and a staircase wide enough to drive a gig up it if it could have turned the corners. A grove of great forest oaks and poplars densely shaded it, and made it look rather gloomy; and the garden, with the old graveyard covered with periwinkle at one end, was almost in front, while the side of the wood—a primeval forest, from which the place took its name—came up so close as to form a strong, dark background. During the war the place, like most others in that neighborhood, suffered greatly, and only a sudden exhibition of spirit on Cousin Fanny's part saved it from a worse fate. After the war it went down; the fields were poor, and grew up in briers and sassafras, and the house was too large and out of repair to keep from decay, the ownership of it being divided between Cousin Fanny and other members of the family. Cousin Fanny had no means whatever, so that it soon was in a bad condition. The rest of the family, as they grew up, went off, compelled by necessity to seek some means of livelihood, and would have taken Cousin Fanny too if she would have gone; but she would not go. They did all they could for her, but she preferred to hang around the old place, and to do what she could with her "mammy," and "old Stephen," her mammy's husband, who alone remained in the quarters. She lived in a part of the house, locking up the rest, and from time to time visited among her friends and relatives, who always received her hospitably. She had an old piece of a mare (which I think she had bought from Stephen), with one eye, three legs, and no mane or tail to speak of, and on which she lavished, without the least perceptible result, care enough to have kept a stable in condition. In a freak of humor she named this animal "Fashion," after a noted racer of the old times, which had been raised in the county, and had beaten the famous Boston in a great race. She always spoke of "Fash" with a tone of real tenderness in her voice, and looked after her, and discussed her ailments, which were always numerous, as if she had been a delicate child. Mounted on this beast, with her bags and bundles, and shawls and umbrella, and a long stick or pole, she used occasionally to make the tour of the neighborhood, and was always really welcomed; because, notwithstanding the trouble she gave, she always stirred things up. As was said once, you could no more have remained dull where she was than you could have dozed with a chinkapin-burr down your back. Her retort was that a chinkapin-burr might be used to rouse people from a lethargy (she had an old maid's tongue). By the younger members of the family she was always welcomed, because she furnished so much fun. She nearly always fetched some little thing to her host—not her hostess—a fowl, or a pat of butter from her one old cow, or something of the kind, because, she said, "Abigail had established the precedent, and she was 'a woman of good understanding'—she understood that feeding and flattery were the way to win men."

She would sometimes have a chicken in a basket hung on the off pummel of her old saddle, because at times she fancied she could not eat anything but chicken soup, and she did "not wish to give trouble." She used to give trouble enough; for it generally turned out that she had heard some one was sick in the neighborhood, and she wanted the soup carried to her. I remember how mad Joe got because she made him go with her to carry a bucket of soup to old Mrs. Ronquist.

Cousin Fanny had the marks of an old maid. She was thin ("scrawny" we used to call her, though I remember now she was quite erect until she grew feeble); her features were fine; her nose was very straight; her hair was brown; and her eyes, which were dark, were weak, so that she had often to wear a green shade. She used to say herself that they were "bad eyes." They had been so ever since the time when she was a young girl, and there had been a very bad attack of scarlet fever at her home, and she had caught it. I think she caught a bad cold with it—sitting up nursing some of the younger children, perhaps—and it had settled in her eyes. She was always very liable to cold.

I believe she had a lover then or about that

time; but her mother had died not long before, and she had some notion of duty to the children, and so discarded him. Of course, as every one said, she 'd much better have married him. I do not suppose he ever could have addressed her. She never would admit that he did, which did not look much like it. She was once spoken of in my presence as "a sore-eyed old maid"—I have forgotten who said it. Yet I can now recall occasions when her eyes, being "better," appeared unusually soft, and, had she not been an old maid, would sometimes have been beautiful—as, for instance, occasionally, when she was playing at the piano in the evenings before the candles were lighted. I recollect particularly once when she was singing an old French love-song. Another time was when on a certain occasion some one was talking about marriages and the reasons which led to or prevented them. She sat quite still and silent, looking out of the window, with her thin hands resting in her lap. Her head was turned away from most of the people, but I was sitting where I could see her, and the light of the evening sky was on her face. It made her look very soft. She lifted up her eyes, and looked far off toward the horizon. I remember it recalled to me, young as I was, the speech I had heard some one once make when I was a little boy, and which I had thought so ridiculous, that "when she was young, before she caught that cold, she was almost beautiful." There was an expression on her face that made me think she ought always to sit looking out of the window at the evening sky. I believe she had brought me some apples that day when she came, and that made me feel kindly toward her. The light on her hair gave it a reddish look, quite auburn. Presently, she withdrew her eyes from the sky, and let them fall into her lap with a sort of long, sighing breath, and slowly interlaced her fingers. The next second some one jocularly fired this question at her: "Well, Cousin Fanny, give us your views," and her expression changed back to that which she ordinarily wore.

"Oh, my views, like other people's, vary from my practice," she said. "It is not views, but experiences, which are valuable in life. When I shall have been married twice I will tell you."

"While there's life there's hope, eh?" hazarded some one; for teasing an old maid, in any way, was held perfectly legitimate.

"Yes, indeed," and she left the room, smiling, and went up-stairs.

This was one of the occasions when her eyes looked well. There were others that I remember, as sometimes when she was in church; sometimes when she was playing with little children; and now and then when, as on that evening, she was sitting still, gazing out of the window. But usually her eyes were weak, and she wore the green shade, which gave her face a peculiar pallor, making her look old, and giving her a pained, invalid expression.

Her dress was one of her peculiarities. Perhaps it was because she made her clothes herself, without being able to see very well. I suppose she did not have much to dress on. I know she used to turn her dresses, and change them around several times. When she had any money she used to squander it, buying dresses for Scroggs's girls or for some one else. She was always scrupulously neat, being quite old-maidish. She said that cleanliness was next to godliness in a man, and in a woman it was on a par with it. I remember once seeing a picture of her as a young girl, as young as Kitty, dressed in a soft white dress, with her hair down over her ears, and some flowers in her dress—that is, it was said to be she; but I did not believe it. To be sure, the flowers looked like it. She always would stick flowers or leaves in her dress, which was thought quite ridiculous. The idea of associating flowers with an old maid! It was as hard as believing she ever was the young girl. It was not, however, her dress, old and often queer and ill-made as it used to be, that was the chief grievance against her. There was a much stronger ground of complaint; she had *nerves!* The word used to be strung out in pronouncing it, with a curve of the lips, as "ner-erves." I don't remember that she herself ever mentioned them; that was the exasperating part of it. She would never say a word; she would just close her thin lips tight, and wear a sort of ill look, as if she were in actual pain. She used to go up-stairs, and shut the door and windows tight, and go to bed, and have mustard-plasters on her temples and the back of her neck; and when she came down, after a day or two, she would have bright red spots burnt on her temples and neck, and would look ill. Of course it was very hard not to be exasperated at this. Then she would creep about as if merely stepping jarred her; would put on a heavy blue veil, and wrap her head up in a shawl, and feel along by the chairs till she got to a seat, and drop back in it, gasping. Why, I have even seen her sit in the room, all swathed up, and with an old parasol over her head to keep out the light, or some such nonsense, as we used to think. It was too ridiculous to us, and we boys used to walk heavily and stumble over chairs — "accidentally," of course — just to make her jump. Sometimes she would even start up and cry out. We had the incontestable proof that it was all "put on;" for if you began to talk to her, and got her interested, she would forget all about her ailments, and would run on and talk and laugh for an hour, until she suddenly remembered, and sank back again in her shawls and pains.

She knew a great deal. In fact, I recall now that she seemed to know more than any woman I have ever been thrown with, and if she had not been an old maid, I am bound to admit that her conversation would have been the most entertaining I ever knew. She lived in a sort of atmosphere of romance and literature; the old writers and their characters were as real to her as we were, and she used to talk about them to us whenever we would let her. Of course, when it came from an old maid, it made a difference. She was not only easily the best French scholar in our region, where the ladies all knew more or less of French, but she was an excellent Latin scholar, which was much less common. I have often lain down before the fire when I was learning my Latin lesson, and read to her, line by line, Cæsar or Ovid or Cicero, as the book might be, and had her render it into English almost as fast as I read. Indeed, I have even seen Horace read to her as she sat in the old rocking-chair after one of her headaches, with her eyes bandaged, and her head swathed in veils and shawls, and she would turn it into not only proper English, but English with a glow and color and rhythm that gave the very life of the odes. This was an exercise we boys all liked and often engaged in—Frank, and Joe, and Doug, and I, and even old Blinky—for, as she used to admit herself, she was aways worrying us to read to her (I believe I read all of Scott's novels to her). Of course this translation helped us as well as gratified her. I do not remember that she was ever too unwell to help us in this way except when she was actually in bed. She was very fond of us boys, and was always ready to take our side and to further our plans in any way whatever. We would get her to steal off with us, and translate our Latin for us by the fire. This, of course, made us rather fond of her. She was so much inclined to take our part and to help us that I remember it used to be said of her as a sort of reproach, "Cousin Fanny always sides with the boys." She used to say it was because she knew how worthless women were. She would say this sort of thing herself, but she was very touchy about women, and never would allow any one else to say anything about them. She had an old maid's temper. I remember that she took Doug up short once for talking about "old maids." She said that for her part she did not mind it the least bit; but she would not allow him to speak so of a large class of her sex which contained some of the best women in the world; that many of them performed work and made sacrifices that the rest of the world knew nothing about. She said the true word for them was the old Saxon term "spinster;" that it proved that they performed the work of the house, and that it was a term of honor of which she was proud. She said that Christ had humbled himself to be born of a Virgin, and that every woman had this honor to sustain. Of course such lectures as that made us call her an old maid all the more. Still, I don't think that being mischievous or teasing her made any difference with her. Frank used to worry her more than any one else, even than Joe, and I am sure she liked him best of all. That may perhaps have been because he was the best-looking of us. She said once that he reminded her of some one she used to know a long time before, when she was young. That must have been a long time before, indeed. He used to tease the life out of her.

She was extraordinarily credulous — would believe anything on earth anyone told her, because, although she had plenty of humor, she herself never would deviate from the absolute truth a moment, even in jest. I do not think she would have told an untruth to save her life. Well, of course we used to play on her to tease her. Frank would tell her the most unbelievable and impossible lies: such as that he thought he saw a mouse yesterday on the back of the sofa she was lying on (this would make her bounce up like a ball), or that he believed he heard—he was not sure—that Mr. Scroggs (the man who had rented her old home) had cut down all the old trees in the yard, and pulled down the house because he wanted the bricks to make brick ovens. This would worry her excessively (she loved every brick in the old house, and often said she would rather live in the kitchen there than in a palace anywhere else), and she would get into such a state of depression that Frank would finally have to tell her that he was just "fooling her."

She used to make him do a good deal of waiting on her in return, and he was the one she used to get to dress old Fashion's back when it was raw, and to put drops in her eyes. He got quite expert at it. She said it was a penalty for his worrying her so.

She was the great musician of the connection. This is in itself no mean praise; for it was the fashion for every musical gift among the girls to be cultivated, and every girl played or sang more or less, some of them very well. But Cousin Fanny was not only this. She had a way of playing that used to make the old piano sound different from itself; and her voice was almost the sweetest I ever heard except one or two on the stage. It was particularly sweet in the evenings, when she sat down at the piano and played. She would not always do it; she either felt "not in the mood," or "not sympathetic," or some such thing. None of the others were that way; the rest could play just as well in the glare of day as in the twilight, and before one person as another; it was, we all knew, just one of Cousin Fanny's old-maid crotchets. When she sat down at the piano and played, her fussiness was all forgotten; her first notes used to be recognized through the house, and people used to stop what they were doing, and come in. Even the children would leave off playing, and come straggling in, tiptoeing as they crossed the floor. Some of the other performers used to play a great deal louder, but we never tiptoed when they played. Cousin Fanny would sit at the piano looking either up or right straight ahead of her, or often with her eyes closed (she never looked at the keys), and the sound used to rise from under her long, thin fingers, sometimes rushing and pouring forth like a deep roar, sometimes ringing out clear like a band of bugles, making the hair move on the head and giving strange tinglings down the back. Then we boys wanted to go forth in the world on fiery, black chargers, like the olden knights, and fight giants and rescue beautiful ladies and poor women. Then again, with her eyes shut, the sound would almost die away, and her fingers would move softly and lingeringly as if they loved the touch of the keys, and hated to leave them; and the sound would come from away far off, and everything would grow quiet and subdued, and the perfume of the roses out of doors would steal in on the air, and the soft breezes would stir the trees, and we were all in love, and wanted to see somebody that we didn't see. And Cousin Fanny was not herself any longer, but we imagined some one else was there. Sometimes she suddenly began to sing (she sang old songs, English or French); her voice might be weak (it all depended on her whims; *she* said, on her health), in that case she always stopped and left the piano; or it might be "in condition." When it was, it was as velvety and mellow as a bell far off, and the old ballads and *chansons* used to fill the twilight. We used even to forget then that she was an old maid. Now and then she sang songs that no one else had ever heard. They were her own; she had composed both the words and the air. At other times she sang the songs of others to her own airs. I remember the first time I ever heard of Tennyson was when, one evening in the twilight, she sang his echo song from "The Princess." The air was her own, and in the refrain you heard perfectly the notes of the bugle, and the echoes answering, "Dying, dying, dying." Boy as I was, I was entranced, and she answered my enthusiasm by turning and repeating the poem. I have often thought since how musical her voice was as she repeated

> Our echoes roll from soul to soul,
> And grow forever and forever.

She had a peculiarly sentimental temperament. As I look back at it all now, she was much given to dwelling upon old-time poems and romances, which we thought very ridiculous in any one, especially in a spinster of forty odd. She would stop and talk about the branch of a tree with the leaves all turning red or yellow or purple in the common way in which, as everyone knows, leaves always turn in the fall; or even about a tangle of briers, scarlet with frost, in a corner of an old worm-fence, keeping us waiting while she fooled around a brier patch with old Blinky, who would just as lief have been in one place as another, so it was out of doors; and even when she reached the house she would still carry on about it, worrying us by telling over again just how the boughs and leaves looked massed against the old gray fence, which she could do till you could see them precisely as they were. She was very aggravating in this way. Sometimes she would even take a pencil or pen and a sheet of paper for old Blinky, and reproduce it. •She could not draw, of course, for she was not a painter; all she could do was to make anything look almost just like it was.

There was one thing about her which excited much talk; I suppose it was only a piece of old-maidism. Of course she was religious. She was really very good. She was considered very high church. I do not think, from my recollection of her, that she really was, or, indeed, that she could have been; but she used to talk that way, and it was said that she was. In fact, it used to be whispered that she was in danger of becoming a Catholic. I believe she had an aunt that was one, and she had visited several times in Norfolk and Baltimore, where it was said there were a good many. I remember she used to defend them, and say she knew a great many very devout ones. And she admitted that she sometimes went to the Catholic church, and found it devotional; the choral service, she said, satisfied something in her soul. It happened to be in the evening that she was talking about this. She sat down at the piano, and played some of the Gregorian chants she had heard, and it had a soothing influence on everyone. Even Joe, the fidgetiest of all, sat quite still through it. She said that some one had said it was the music that the angels sing in heaven around the great white throne, and there was no other sacred music like it. But she played another thing that evening which she said was worthy to be played with it. It had some chords in it that I remembered long afterward. Years afterward I heard it played the same way in the twilight by one who is a blessed saint in heaven, and may be playing it there now. It was from Chopin. She even said that evening, under the impulse of her enthusiasm, that she did not see, except that it might be abused, why the crucifix should not be retained by all Christian churches, as it enabled some persons not gifted with strong imaginations to have a more vivid realization of the crucified Saviour. This, of course, was going too far, and it created considerable excitement in the family, and led to some very serious talk being given her, in which the second commandment figured largely. It was considered as carrying old-maidism to an extreme length. For some time afterward she was rather discountenanced. In reality, I think what some said was true: it was simply that she was emotional, as old maids are apt to be. She once said that many women have the nun's instinct largely developed, and sigh for the peace of the cloister.

She seemed to be very fond of artists. She had the queerest tastes, and had, or had had when she was young, one or two friends who, I believe, claimed to be something of that kind; she used to talk about them to old Blinky. But it seemed to us from what she said that artists never did any work; just spent their time lounging around, doing nothing, and daubing paint on their canvas with brushes like a painter, or chiselling and chopping rocks like a mason. One of these friends of hers was a young man from Norfolk who had made a good many things. He was killed or died in the war; so he had not been quite ruined; was worth something anyhow as a soldier. One of his things was a Psyche, and Cousin Fanny used to talk a good deal about it; she said it was fine, was a work of genius. She had even written some verses about it. She repeated them to me once, and I wrote them down. Here they are:

TO GALT'S PSYCHE.

Well art thou called the soul;
   For as I gaze on thee,
My spirit, past control,
   Springs up in ecstasy.

Thou canst not be dead stone;
   For o'er thy lovely face,
Softer than music's tone,
   I see the spirit's grace.

The wild æolian lyre
   Is but a silken string,
Till summer winds inspire,
   And softest music bring.

> Psyche, thou wast but stone
> Till his inspiring came:
> The sculptor's hand alone
> Made not that soul-touched frame.

They have lain by me for years, and are pretty good for one who didn't write. I think, however, she was young when she addressed them to the "soul-touched" work of the young sculptor, who laid his genius and everything at Virginia's feet. They were friends, I believe, when she was a girl, before she caught that cold, and her eyes got bad.

Among her eccentricities was her absurd cowardice. She was afraid of cows, afraid of horses, afraid even of sheep. And bugs, and anything that crawled, used to give her a fit. If we drove her anywhere, and the horses cut up the least bit, she would jump out and walk, even in the mud; and I remember once seeing her cross the yard, where a young cow that had a calf asleep in the weeds, over in a corner beyond her, started toward it at a little trot with a whimper of motherly solicitude. Cousin Fanny took it into her head that the cow was coming at her, and just screamed, and sat down flat on the ground, carrying on as if she were a baby. Of course, we boys used to tease her, and tell her the cows were coming after her. You could not help teasing anybody like that.

I do not see how she managed to do what she did when the enemy got to Woodside in the war. That was quite remarkable, considering what a coward she was. During 1864 the Yankees on a raid got to her house one evening in the summer. As it happened, a young soldier, one of her cousins (she had no end of cousins), had got a leave of absence, and had come there sick with fever just the day before (the house was always a sort of hospital). He was in the boys' room in bed when the Yankees arrived, and they were all around the house before she knew it. She went downstairs to meet them. They had been informed by one of the negroes that Cousin Charlie was there, and they told her that they wanted him. She told them they could not get him. They asked her, "Why? Is he not there?" (I heard her tell of it once.) She said:

"You know, I thought when I told them they could not get him that they would go away, but when they asked me if he was not there, of course I could not tell them a story; so I said I declined to answer impertinent questions. You know poor Charlie was at that moment lying curled up under the bed in the boys' room with a roll of carpet a foot thick around him, and it was as hot as an oven. Well, they insisted on going through the house, and I let them go all through the lower stories; but when they started up the staircase I was ready for them. I had always kept, you know, one of papa's old horse-pistols as a protection. Of course, it was not loaded. I would not have had it loaded for anything in the world. I always kept it safely locked up, and I was dreadfully afraid of it even then. But you have no idea what a moral support it gave me, and I used to unlock the drawer every afternoon to see if it was still there all right, and then lock it again, and put the key away carefully. Well, as it happened, I had just been looking at it — which I called 'inspecting my garrison.' I used to feel just like Lady Margaret in Tillietudlam Castle. Well, I had just been looking at it that afternoon when I heard the Yankees were coming, and by a sudden inspiration—I cannot tell for my life how I did it—I seized the pistol, and hid it under my apron. I held on to it with both hands, I was so afraid of it, and all the time those wretches were going through the rooms down-stairs I was quaking with terror. But when they started up the stairs I had a new feeling. I knew they were bound to get poor

Charlie if he had not melted and run away,—no, he would never have run away; I mean evaporated,—and I suddenly ran up the stairway a few steps before them, and, hauling out my big pistol, pointed it at them, and told them that if they came one step higher I would certainly pull the trigger. I could not say I would shoot, for it was not loaded. Well, do you know, they stopped! They stopped dead still. I declare I was so afraid the old pistol would go off, though, of course, I knew it was not loaded, that I was just quaking. But as soon as they stopped, I began to attack. I remembered my old grandmother and her scissors, and, like General Jackson, I followed up my advantage. I descended the steps, brandishing my pistol with both hands, and abusing them with all my might. I was so afraid they might ask if it was loaded. But they really thought I would shoot them (you know men have not liked to be slain by a woman since the time of Abimelech), and they actually ran down the steps, with me after them, and I got them all out of the house. Then I locked the door and barred it, and ran up-stairs and had such a cry over Charlie. [That was like an old maid.] Afterwards they were going to burn the house, but I got hold of their colonel, who was not

My Cousin Fanny

there at first, and made him really ashamed of himself; for I told him we were nothing but a lot of poor defenceless women and a sick boy. He said he thought I was right well defended, as I had held a company at bay. He finally promised that if I would give him some music he would not go up-stairs. So I paid that for my ransom, and a bitter ransom it was too, I can tell you, singing for a Yankee! But I gave him a dose of Confederate songs, I promise you. He asked me to sing the 'Star Spangled Banner;' but I told him I would not do it if he burnt the house down with me in it—though it was inspired by my cousin, Armistead. Then he asked me to sing 'Home, Sweet Home,' and I did that, and he actually had tears in his eyes —the hypocrite! He had very fine eyes, too. I think I did sing it well, though. I cried a little myself, thinking of the old house being so nearly burnt. There was a young doctor there, a surgeon, a really nice-looking fellow for a Yankee; I made him feel ashamed of himself, I tell you. I told him I had no doubt he had a good mother and sister up at home, and to think of his coming and warring on poor women. And they really placed a guard over the house for me while they were there."

This she actually did. With her old empty horse-pistol she cleared the house of the mob, and then vowed that if they burned the house she would burn up in it, and finally saved it by singing "Home, Sweet Home," for the colonel. She could not have done much better even if she had not been an old maid.

I did not see much of her after I grew up. I moved away from the old county. Most others did the same. It had been desolated by the war, and got poorer and poorer. With an old maid's usual crankiness and inability to adapt herself to the order of things, Cousin Fanny remained behind. She refused to come away; said, I believe, she had to look after the old place, mammy, and Fash, or some such nonsense. I think she had some idea that the church would go down, or that the poor people around would miss her, or something equally unpractical. Anyhow, she stayed behind, and lived for quite awhile the last of her connection in the county. Of course all did the best they could for her, and had she gone to live around with her relatives, as they wished her to do, they would have borne with her and supported her. But she said no; that a single woman ought never to live in any house but her father's or her own; and we could not do anything with her. She was so proud she would not take money as a gift from anyone, not even from her nearest relatives.

Her health got rather poor—not unnaturally, considering the way she divided her time between doctoring herself and fussing after sick people in all sorts of weather. With the fancifulness of her kind, she finally took it into her head that she must consult a doctor in New York. Of course, no one but an old maid would have done this; the home doctors were good enough for everyone else. Nothing would do, however, but she must go to New York; so, against the advice of everyone, she wrote to a cousin who was living there to meet her, and with her old wraps, and cap, and bags, and bundles, and stick, and umbrella, she started. The lady met her; that is, went to meet her, but failed to find her at the station, and supposing that she had not come, or had taken some other railroad, which she was likely to do, returned home, to find her in bed, with her "things" piled up on the floor. Some gentleman had come across her in Washington, holding the right train while she insisted on taking the wrong route, and had taken compassion on her, and not only escorted her to New York, but had taken her and all her parcels and brought her to her destination, where she had at once retired.

"He was a most charming man, my dear," she said to her cousin, who told me of it afterward in narrating her eccentricities; "and to think of it, I don't believe I had looked in a glass all day, and when I got here, my cap had somehow got twisted around and was perched right over my left ear, making me look a perfect fright. He told me his name, but I have forgotten it, of course. But he was such a gentleman, and to think of his being a Yankee! I told him I hated all Yankees, and he just laughed, and did not mind my stick, nor old umbrella, nor bundles a bit. You'd have thought my old cap was a Parisian bonnet. I will not believe he was a Yankee."

Well, she went to see the doctor, the most celebrated in New York—at the infirmary, of course, for she was too poor to go to his office; one consultation would have taken every cent she had—her cousin went with her, and told me of it. She said that when she came downstairs to go she never saw such a sight. On her head she had her blue cap, and her green shade and her veil, and her shawl; and she had the old umbrella and long stick, which she had brought from the country, and a large pillow under her arm, because she "knew she was going to faint." So they started out, but it was a slow procession. The noise and bustle of the street dazed her, her cousin fancied, and every now and then she would clutch her companion and declare she must go back or she should faint. At every street-crossing she insisted upon having a policeman to help her over, or, in default of that, she would stop some man and ask him to escort her across, which, of course, he would do, thinking her crazy.

Finally they reached the infirmary, where there were already a large number of patients, and many more came in afterwards. Here she shortly established an acquaintance with several strangers. She had to wait an hour or more for her turn, and then insisted that several who had come in after her should go in before her, because she said the poor things looked so tired. This would have gone on indefinitely, her cousin said, if she had not finally dragged her into the doctor's room. There the first thing that she did was to insist that she must lie down, she was so faint, and her pillow was brought into requisition. The doctor humored her, and waited on her. Her friend started to tell him about her, but the doctor said, "I prefer to have her tell me herself." She presently began to tell, the doctor sitting quietly by listening and seeming to be much interested. He gave her some prescription, and told her to come again next day, and when she went he sent for her ahead of her turn, and after that made her come to his office at his private house, instead of to the infirmary, as at first. He turned out to be the surgeon who had been at her house with the Yankees during the war. He was very kind to her. I suppose he had never seen anyone like her. She used to go every day, and soon dispensed with her friend's escort, finding no difficulty in getting about. Indeed, she came to be known on the streets she passed through, and on the cars she travelled by, and people guided her. Several times as she was taking the wrong car men stopped her, and said, to her, "Madam, yours is the red car." She said, sure enough it was, but she never could divine how they knew. She addressed the conductors as, "My dear sir," and made them help her not only off, but quite to the sidewalk, when she thanked them, and said "Good-by," as if she had been at home. She said she did this on principle, for it was such a good thing to teach them to help a feeble woman. Next time they would expect to do it, and after a while it would become a habit. She said no one knew what terror women had of being run over and trampled on.

She was, as I have said, an awful coward. She used to stand still on the edge of the street and look up and down both ways ever so long, then go out in the street and stand still, look both ways and then run back; or as like as not start on and turn and run back after she was more than half way across, and so get into real danger. One day, as she was passing along, a driver had in his cart an old bag-of-bones of a horse, which he was beating to make him pull up the hill, and Cousin Fanny, with an old maid's meddlesomeness, pushed out into the street and caught hold of him and made him stop, which of course collected a crowd, and just as she was coming back a little cart came rattling along, and though she was in no earthly danger, she ran so to get out of the way of the horse that she tripped and fell down in the street and hurt herself. So much for cowardice.

The doctor finally told her that she had nothing the matter with her, except something with her nerves and, I believe, her spine, and that she wanted company (you see she was a good deal alone). He said it was the first law of health ever laid down, that it was not good for man to be alone; that loneliness is a specific disease. He said she wanted occupation, some sort of work to interest her, and make her forget her aches and ailments. He suggested missionary work of some kind. This was one of the worst things he could have told her, for there was no missionary work to be had where she lived. Besides, she could not have done missionary work; she had never done anything in her life; she was always wasting her time pottering about the country on her old horse, seeing sick old darkies or poor people in the pines. No matter how bad the weather was, nor how deep the roads, she would go prowling around to see some old "aunty" or "uncle," in their out-of-the-way cabins, or somebody's sick child. I have met her on old Fashion in the rain, toiling along in roads that were knee-deep, to get the doctor to come to see some sick person, or to get a dose of physic from the depot. How could she have done any missionary work?

I believe she repaid the doctor for his care of her by sending him a charity patient to look after—Scroggs's eldest girl, who was bedridden or something. Cousin Fanny had a fancy that she was musical. I never knew how it was arranged. I think the doctor sent the money down to have the child brought on to New York for him to see. I suppose Cousin Fanny turned beggar, and asked him. I know she told him the child was the daughter of "a friend" of hers (a curious sort of friend Scroggs was, a drunken creature, who had done everything he could to pain her), and she took a great deal of trouble to get her to the train, lending old Fashion to haul her, which was a great deal more than lending herself; and the doctor treated her in New York for three months without any charge, till, I believe, the child got better. Old maids do not mind giving people trouble.

She hung on at the old place as long as she could, but it had to be sold, and finally she had to leave it; though, I believe, even after it was sold she tried boarding for a while with Scroggs, the former tenant, who had bought it. He treated her so badly that finally she had to leave, and boarded around. I believe the real cause was she caught him ploughing with old Fashion.

After that I do not know exactly what she did. I heard that though the parish was vacant she had a Sunday-school at the old church, and so kept the church open; and that she used to play the wheezy old organ and teach the poor children the chants; but as they grew up they all joined another Church; they had a new organ there. I do not know just how she got on. I was surprised to hear finally that she was dead—had been dead since Christmas. It had never occurred to me that she would die. She had been dying so long that I had almost come to regard her as immortal, and as a necessary part of the old county and its associations.

I fell in some time afterwards with a young doctor from the old county, who, I found, had attended her, and I made some inquiries about her. He told me that she died Christmas night. She came to his house on her old mare, in the rain and snow the night before, to get him to go to see someone, some "friend" of hers who was sick. He said she had more sick friends than anyone he ever knew; he told her that he was sick himself and could not go; but she was so importunate that he promised to go next morning (she was always very worrying). He said she was wet and shivering then (she never had any idea about really protecting herself), and that she appeared to have a wretched cold. She had been riding all day seeing about a Christmas-tree for the poor children. He urged her to stop and spend the night, but she insisted that she must go on, though it was nearly dark and raining hard, and the roads would have mired a cat (she was always self-willed). Next day he went to see the sick woman, and when he arrived he found her in one bed and Cousin Fanny in another, in the same room. When he had examined the patient, he turned and asked Cousin Fanny what was the matter with her. "Oh, just a little cold, a little trouble in the chest, as Theodore Hook said," she replied. "But I know how to doctor myself." Something about her voice struck him. He went over to her and looked at her, and found her suffering from acute pneumonia. He at once set to work on her. He took the other patient up in his arms and carried her into another room, where he told her that Cousin Fanny was a desperately ill woman. "She was actually dying then, sir," he said to me, "and she died that night. When she arrived at the place the night before, which was not until after nine o'clock, she had gone to the stable herself to put up her old mare, or rather to see that she was fed—she always did that—so when she got into the house she was wet and chilled through, and she had to go to bed. She must have had on wet clothes," he said.

I asked him if she knew she was going to die. He said he did not think she did; that he did not tell her, and she talked about nothing except her Christmas-tree and the people she wanted to see. He heard her praying in the night, "and, by the way," he said, "she mentioned you. She shortly became rather delirious, and wandered a good deal, talking of things that must have happened when she was young; spoke of going to see her mother somewhere. The last thing she ever said was something about fashion, which," he said, "showed how ingrained is vanity in the female mind." The doctor knows something of human nature. He concluded what he had to say with, "She was in some respects a very remarkable woman—if she had not been an old maid. I do not suppose that she ever drew a well breath in her life. Not that I think old maids cannot be very acceptable women," he apologized. "They are sometimes very useful." The doctor was a rather enlightened man.

Some of her relatives got there in time for the funeral, and a good many of the poor people came; and she was carried in a little old spring wagon, drawn by Fashion, through the snow, to the old home place, where Scroggs very kindly let them dig the grave, and was buried there in the old graveyard in the garden, in a vacant space just beside her mother, with the children around her. I really miss her a great deal. The other boys say they do the same. I suppose it is the trouble she used to give us.

The old set are all doing well. Doug is a professor. He says the word "spinster" gave him a twist to philology. Old Blinky is in Paris. He had a picture in the salon last year, an autumn landscape, called "Le Côté du Bois." I believe the translation of that is "The Woodside." His coloring is said to be nature itself. To think of old Blinky being a great artist! Little Kitty is now a big girl, and is doing finely at school. I have told her she must not be an old maid. Joe is a preacher with a church in the purlieus of a large city. I was there not long ago. He had a choral service. The Gregorian music carried me back to old times. He preached on the text, "I was sick, and ye visited me." It was such a fine sermon, and he had such a large congregation, that I asked why he did not go to a finer church. He said he was "carrying soup to Mrs. Ronquist." By the way, his organist was a splendid musician. She introduced herself to me. It was Scroggs's daughter. She is married, and can walk as well as I can. She had a little girl with her that I think she called "Fanny." I do not think that was Mrs. Scroggs's name.

Frank is now a doctor, or rather a surgeon, in the same city with Joe, and becoming very distinguished. The other day he performed a great operation, saving a woman's life, which was in all the papers. He said to an interviewer that he became a surgeon from dressing a sore on an old mare's back. I wonder what he was talking about? He is about to start a woman's hospital for poor women. Cousin Fanny would have been glad of that; she was always proud of Frank. She would as likely as not have quoted that verse from Tennyson's song about the echoes. She sleeps now under the myrtle at Scroggs's. I have often thought of what that doctor said about her: that she would have been a very remarkable woman, if she had not been an old maid—I mean, a spinster.

The Burial of the Guns

THE BURIAL OF THE GUNS

LEE surrendered the remnant of his army at Appomattox, April 9, 1865, and yet a couple of days later the old Colonel's battery lay intrenched right in the mountain-pass where it had halted three days before. Two weeks previously it had been detailed with a light division sent to meet and repel a force which it was understood was coming in by way of the southwest valley to strike Lee in the rear of his long line from Richmond to Petersburg. It had done its work. The mountain-pass had been seized and held, and the Federal force had not gotten by that road within the blue rampart which guarded on that side the heart of Virginia. This pass, which was the key to the main line of passage over the mountains, had been assigned by the commander of the division to the old Colonel and his old battery, and they had held it. The position taken by the battery had been chosen with a soldier's eye. A better place could not have been selected to

The Burial of the Guns

hold the pass. It was its highest point, just where the road crawled over the shoulder of the mountain along the limestone cliff, a hundred feet sheer above the deep river, where its waters had cut their way in ages past, and now lay deep and silent, as if resting after their arduous toil before they began to boil over the great bowlders which filled the bed a hundred or more yards below.

The little plateau at the top guarded the descending road on either side for nearly a mile, and the mountain on the other side of the river was the centre of a clump of rocky, heavily timbered spurs, so inaccessible that no feet but those of wild animals or of the hardiest hunter had ever climbed it. On the side of the river on which the road lay, the only path out over the mountain except the road itself was a charcoal-burner's track, dwindling at times to a footway known only to the mountain-folk, which a picket at the top could hold against an army. The position, well defended, was impregnable, and it was well defended. This the general of the division knew when he detailed the old Colonel and gave him his order to hold the pass until relieved, and not let his guns fall into the hands of the enemy. He knew both the Colonel and his battery. The battery was one of the oldest in the army. It had been in the service since April, 1861, and its commander had come to be known as "The Wheel Horse of his division." He was, perhaps, the oldest officer of his rank in his branch of the service. Although he had bitterly opposed secession, and was many years past the age of service when the war came on, yet as soon as the President called on the State for her quota of troops to coerce South Carolina, he had raised and uniformed an artillery company, and offered it, not to the President of the United States, but to the Governor of Virginia.

It is just at this point that he suddenly looms up to me as a soldier; the relation he never wholly lost to me afterward, though I knew him for many, many years of peace. His gray coat with the red facing and the bars on the collar; his military cap; his gray flannel shirt—it was the first time I ever saw him wear anything but immaculate linen—his high boots;. his horse caparisoned with a black, high-peaked saddle, with crupper and breast-girth, instead of the light English hunting-saddle to which I had been accustomed, all come before me now as if it were but the other day. I remember but little beyond it, yet I remember, as if it were yesterday, his leaving home, and the scenes which immediately preceded it ; the excitement created by the news of the President's call for troops ; the unanimous judgment that it meant war ; the immediate determination of the old Colonel, who had hitherto opposed secession, that it must be met ; the suppressed agitation on the plantation, attendant upon the tender of his services and the Governor's acceptance of them. The prompt and continuous work incident to the enlistment of the men, the bustle of preparation, and all the scenes of that time, come before me now. It turned the calm current of the life of an old and placid country neighborhood, far from any city or centre, and stirred it into a boiling torrent, strong enough, or fierce enough to cut its way and join the general torrent which was bearing down and sweeping everything before it. It seemed but a minute before the quiet old plantation, in which the harvest, the corn-shucking, and the Christmas holidays alone marked the passage of the quiet seasons, and where a strange carriage or a single horseman coming down the big road was an event in life, was turned into a depot of war-supplies, and the neighborhood became a parade-ground. The old Colonel, not a colonel yet, nor even a captain, except by brevet, was on his horse by daybreak and off on his rounds

The Burial of the Guns

through the plantations and the pines enlisting his company. The office in the yard, heretofore one in name only, became one now in reality, and a table was set out piled with papers, pens, ink, books of tactics and regulation, at which men were accepted and enrolled. Soldiers seemed to spring from the ground, as they did from the sowing of the dragon's teeth in the days of Cadmus. Men came up the high road or down the paths across the fields, sometimes singly, but oftener in little parties of two or three, and, asking for the Captain, entered the office as private citizens and came out soldiers enlisted for the war. There was nothing heard of on the plantation except fighting; white and black, all were at work, and all were eager; the servants contended for the honor of going with their master; the women flocked to the house to assist in the work of preparation, cutting out and making under-clothes, knitting socks, picking lint, preparing bandages, and sewing on uniforms; for many of the men who had enlisted were of the poorest class, far too poor to furnish anything themselves, and their equipment had to be contributed mainly by wealthier neighbors. The work was carried on at night as well as by day, for the occasion was urgent. Meantime the men were being drilled by the Captain and his lieutenants, who had been militia officers of old. We were carried to see the drill at the cross-roads, and a brave sight it seemed to us: the lines marching and countermarching in the field, with the horses galloping as they wheeled amid clouds of dust, at the hoarse commands of the excited officers, and the roadside lined with spectators of every age and condition. I recall the arrival of the messenger one night, with the telegraphic order to the Captain to report with his company at "Camp Lee" immediately; the hush in the parlor that attended its reading; then the forced beginning of the conversation afterwards in a somewhat strained and unnatural key, and the Captain's quick and decisive outlining of his plans.

Within the hour a dozen messengers were on their way in various directions to notify the members of the command of the summons, and to deliver the order for their attendance at a given point next day. It seemed that a sudden and great change had come. It was the actual appearance of what had hitherto only been theoretical—war. The next morning the Captain, in full uniform, took leave of the assembled plantation, with a few solemn words commending all he left behind to God, and galloped away up the big road to join and lead his battery to the war, and to be gone just four years.

Within a month he was on "the Peninsula" with Magruder, guarding Virginia on the east against the first attack. His camp was first at Yorktown and then on Jamestown Island, the honor having been assigned his battery of guarding the oldest cradle of the race on this continent. It was at "Little Bethel" that his guns were first trained on the enemy, and that the battery first saw what they had to do, and from this time until the middle of April, 1865, they were in service, and no battery saw more service or suffered more in it. Its story was a part of the story of the Southern Army in Virginia. The Captain was a rigid disciplinarian, and his company had more work to do than most new companies. A pious churchman, of the old puritanical type not uncommon to Virginia, he looked after the spiritual as well as the physical welfare of his men, and his chaplain or he read prayers at the head of his company every morning during the war. At first he was not popular with the men, he made the duties of camp life so onerous to them, it was "nothing but drilling and praying all the time," they said. But he had not commanded very long before they came to know the stuff that was in him. He had not been in service a year before he had had four horses shot under him, and when later on he was offered the command of a battalion, the old company petitioned to be one of his batteries, and still remained under his command. Before the first year was out the battery had, through its own elements, and the discipline of the Captain, become a cohesive force, and a distinct integer in the Army of Northern Virginia. Young farmer recruits knew of its prestige and expressed preference for it of many batteries of rapidly growing or grown reputation. Owing to its high stand, the old and clumsy guns with which it had started out were taken from it, and in their place was presented a battery of four fine, brass, twelve-pound Napoleons of the newest and most approved kind, and two three-inch Parrotts, all captured. The men were as pleased with them as children with new toys. The care and attention needed to keep them in prime order broke the monotony of camp life. They soon had abundant opportunities to test their power. They worked admirably, carried far, and were extraordinarily accurate in their aim. The men from admiration of their guns grew to have first a pride in, and then an affection for, them, and gave them nicknames as they did their comrades; the four Napoleons being dubbed, "The Evangelists," and the two rifles being "The Eagle," because of its scream and force, and "The Cat," because when it became hot from rapid firing "It jumped," they said, "like a cat." From many a hill-top in Virginia, Maryland, and Pennsylvania "The Evangelists" spoke their hoarse message of battle and death, "The Eagle" screamed her terrible note, and "The Cat" jumped as she spat her deadly shot from her hot throat. In the Valley of Virginia; on the levels of Henrico and Hanover; on the slopes of Manassas; in the woods of Chancellorsville; on the heights of Fredericksburg; at Antietam and Gettysburg; in the Spottsylvania wilderness, and again on the Hanover levels and on the lines before Petersburg, the old guns through nearly four years roared from fiery throats their deadly messages. The history of the battery was bound up with the history of Lee's army. A rivalry sprang up among the detachments of the different guns, and their several records were jealously kept. The number of duels each gun was in was carefully counted, every scar got in battle was treasured, and the men around their camp-fires, at their scanty messes, or on the march, bragged of them among themselves

The Burial of the Guns

and avouched them as witnesses. New recruits coming in to fill the gaps made by the killed and disabled, readily fell in with the common mood and caught the spirit like a contagion. It was not an uncommon thing for a wheel to be smashed in by a shell, but if it happened to one gun oftener than to another there was envy. Two of the Evangelists seemed to be especially favored in this line, while the Cat was so exempt as to become the subject of some derision. The men stood by the guns till they were knocked to pieces, and when the fortune of the day went against them, had with their own hands oftener than once saved them after most of their horses were killed.

This had happened in turn to every gun, the men at times working like beavers in mud up to their thighs and under a murderous fire to get their guns out. Many a man had been killed tugging at trail or wheel when the day was against them; but not a gun had ever been lost. At last the evil day arrived. At Winchester a sudden and impetuous charge for a while swept everything before it, and carried the knoll where the old battery was posted; but all the guns were got out by the toiling and rapidly dropping men, except the Cat, which was captured with its entire detachment working at it until they were surrounded and knocked from the piece by cavalrymen. Most of the men who were not killed were retaken before the day was over, with many guns; but the Cat was lost. She remained in the enemy's hands and probably was being turned against her old comrades and lovers. The company was inconsolable. The death of comrades was too natural and common a thing to depress the men beyond what such occurrences necessarily did; but to lose a gun! It was like losing the old Colonel; it was worse: a gun was ranked as a brigadier; and the Cat was equal to a major-general. The other guns seemed lost without her; the Eagle especially, which generally went next to her, appeared to the men to have a lonely and subdued air. The battery was no longer the same: it seemed broken and depleted, shrunken to a mere section. It was worse than Cold Harbor, where over half the men were killed or wounded. The old Captain, now Colonel of the battalion, appreciated the loss and apprehended its effect on the men as much as they themselves did, and application was made for a gun to take the place of the lost piece; but there was none to be had, as the men said they had known all along. It was added — perhaps by a department clerk—that if they wanted a gun to take the place of the one they had lost, they had better capture it. "By ——, we will," they said—adding epithets, intended for the department clerk in his "bomb-proof," not to be printed in this record—and they did. For some time afterwards in every engagement into which they got there used to be speculation among them as to whether the Cat were not there on the other side; some of the men swearing they could tell her report, and even going to the rash length of offering bets on her presence.

By one of those curious coincidences, as strange as anything in fiction, a new general had, in 1864, come down across the Rapidan to take Richmond, and the old battery had found a hill-top in the line in which Lee's army lay stretched across "the Wilderness" country to stop him. The day, though early in May, was a hot one, and the old battery, like most others, had suffered fearfully. Two of the guns had had wheels cut down by shells and the men had been badly cut up; but the fortune of the day had been with Lee, and a little before nightfall, after a terrible fight, there was a rapid advance, Lee's infantry sweeping everything before it, and the artillery, after opening the way for the charge, pushing along with it; now unlimbering as some vantage-ground was gained, and using canister with deadly effect; now driving ahead again so rapidly that it was mixed up with the muskets when the long line of breastworks was carried with a rush, and a line of guns were caught still hot from their rapid work. As the old battery, with lathered horses and smoke-grimed men, swung up the crest and unlimbered on the captured breastwork, a cheer went up which was heard even above the long general yell of the advancing line, and for a moment half the men in the battery crowded together around some object on the edge of the redoubt, yelling like madmen. The next instant they divided, and there was the Cat, smoke-grimed and blood-stained and still sweating hot from her last fire, being dragged from her muddy ditch by as many men as could get hold of trail-rope or wheel, and rushed into her old place beside the Eagle, in time to be double-shotted with canister to the muzzle, and to pour it from among her old comrades into her now retiring former masters. Still, she had a new carriage, and her record was lost, while those of the other guns had been faithfully kept by the men. This made a difference in her position for which even the bullets in her wheels did not wholly atone; even Harris, the sergeant of her detachment, felt that.

It was only a few days later, however, that abundant atonement was made. The new general did not retire across the Rapidan after his first defeat, and a new battle had to be fought: a battle, if anything, more furious, more terrible than the first, when the dead filled the trenches and covered the fields. He simply marched by the left flank, and Lee marching by the right flank to head him, flung himself upon him again at Spottsylvania Court-House. That day the Cat, standing in her place behind the new and temporary breastwork thrown up when the battery was posted, had the felloes of her wheels, which showed above the top of the bank, entirely cut away by Minie-bullets, so that when she jumped in the recoil her wheels smashed and let her down. This covered all old scores. The other guns had been cut down by shells or solid shot; but never before had one been gnawed down by musket-balls. From this time all through the campaign the Cat held her own beside her brazen and bloody sisters, and in the cold trenches before Petersburg that winter, when the new general—Starvation—had joined the one already there, she made her bloody mark as often as any gun on the long lines.

Thus the old battery had come to be known, as its old commander, now colonel of a battalion, had come to be known by those in yet higher command. And when in the opening spring of 1865 it became apparent to the leaders of both armies that the long line could not longer be held if a force should enter behind it, and, sweeping the one partially unswept portion of Virginia, cut the railways in the southwest, and a man was wanted to command the artillery in the expedition sent to meet this force, it was not remarkable that the old Colonel and his battalion should be selected for the work. The force sent out was but small; for the long line was worn to a thin one in those days, and great changes were taking place, the consequences of which were known only to the commanders. In a few days the commander of the expedition found that he must divide his small force for a time, at least, to accomplish his purpose, and sending the old Colonel with one battery of artillery to guard one pass, must push on over the mountain by another way to meet the expected force, if possible, and repel it before it crossed the farther range. Thus the old battery, on an April evening of 1865, found it-

The Burial of the Guns

self toiling alone up the steep mountain road which leads above the river to the gap, which formed the chief pass in that part of the Blue Ridge. Both men and horses looked, in the dim and waning light of the gray April day, rather like shadows of the beings they represented than the actual beings themselves. And anyone seeing them as they toiled painfully up, the thin horses floundering in the mud, and the men, often up to their knees, tugging at the sinking wheels, now stopping to rest, and always moving so slowly that they seemed scarcely to advance at all, might have thought them the ghosts of some old battery lost from some long gone and forgotten war on that deep and desolate mountain road. Often, when they stopped, the blowing of the horses and the murmuring of the river in its bed below were the only sounds heard, and the tired voices of the men when they spoke among themselves seemed hardly more articulate sounds than they. Then the voice of the mounted figure on the roan horse half hidden in the mist would cut in, clear and inspiring, in a tone of encouragement more than of command, and everything would wake up: the drivers would shout and crack their whips; the horses would bend themselves on the collars and flounder in the mud; the men would spring once more to the mud-clogged wheels, and the slow ascent would begin again.

The orders to the Colonel, as has been said, were brief: To hold the pass until he received further instructions, and not to lose his guns. To be ordered, with him, was to obey. The last streak of twilight brought them to the top of the pass; his soldier's instinct and a brief recognizance made earlier in the day told him that this was his place, and before daybreak next morning the point was as well fortified as a night's work by weary and supperless men could make it. A prettier spot could not have been found for the purpose; a small plateau, something over an acre in extent, where a charcoal-burner's hut had once stood, lay right at the top of the pass. It was a little higher on either side than in the middle, where a small brook, along which the charcoal-burner's track was yet visible, came down from the wooded mountain above, thus giving a natural crest to aid the fortification on either side, with open space for the guns, while the edge of the wood coming down from the mountain afforded shelter for the camp.

As the battery was unsupported it had to rely on itself for everything, a condition which most soldiers by this time were accustomed to.

The Burial of the Guns

A dozen or so of rifles were in the camp, and with these pickets were armed and posted. The pass had been seized none too soon; a scout brought in the information before nightfall that the invading force had crossed the farther range before that sent to meet it could get there, and taking the nearest road had avoided the main body opposing it, and been met only by a rapidly moving detachment, nothing more than a scouting party, and now were advancing rapidly on the road on which they were posted, evidently meaning to seize the pass and cross the mountain at this point. The day was Sunday; a beautiful Spring Sunday; but it was no Sabbath for the old battery. All day the men worked, making and strengthening their redoubt to guard the pass, and by the next morning, with the old battery at the top, it was impregnable. They were just in time. Before noon their vedettes brought in word that the enemy were ascending the mountain, and the sun had hardly turned when the advance guard rode up, came within range of the picket, and were fired on.

It was apparent that they supposed the force there only a small one, for they retired and soon came up again reinforced in some numbers, and a sharp little skirmish ensued, hot enough to make them more prudent afterwards, though the picket retired up the mountain. This gave them encouragement and probably misled them, for they now advanced boldly. They saw the redoubt on the crest as they came on, and unlimbering a section or two, flung a few shells up at it, which either fell short or passed over without doing material damage. None of the guns was allowed to respond, as the distance was too great with the ammunition the battery had, and, indifferent as it was, it was too precious to be wasted in a duel at an ineffectual range. Doubtless deceived by this, the enemy came on in force, being obliged by the character of the ground to keep almost entirely to the road, which really made them advance in column. The battery waited. Under orders of the Colonel the guns standing in line were double-shotted with canister, and, loaded to the muzzle, were trained down to sweep the road at from four to five hundred yards' distance. And when the column reached this point the six guns, aimed by old and skilful gunners, at a given word swept road and mountain-side with a storm of leaden hail. It was a fire no mortal man could stand up against, and the practised gunners rammed their pieces full again, and before the smoke had cleared or the reverberation had died away among the mountains, had fired the guns again and yet again. The road was cleared of living things when the draught setting down the river drew the smoke away; but it was no discredit to the other force; for no army that was ever uniformed could stand against that battery in that pass. Again and again the attempt was made to get a body of men up under cover of the woods and rocks on the mountain-side, while the guns below utilized their better ammunition from longer range; but it was useless. Although one of the lieutenants and several men were killed in the skirmish, and a number more were wounded, though not severely, the old battery commanded the mountain-side, and its skilful gunners swept it at every point the foot of man could scale. The sun went down flinging his last flame on a victorious battery still crowning the mountain pass. The dead were buried by night in a corner of the little plateau, borne to their last bivouac on the old gun-carriages which they had stood by so often—which the men said would "sort of ease their minds."

The next day the fight was renewed, and with the same result. The old battery in its position was unconquerable. Only one fear

The Burial of the Guns

now faced them; their ammunition was getting as low as their rations; another such day or half-day would exhaust it. A sergeant was sent back down the mountain to try to get more, or, if not, to get tidings. The next day it was supposed the fight would be renewed; and the men waited, alert, eager, vigilant, their spirits high, their appetite for victory whetted by success. The men were at their breakfast, or what went for breakfast, scanty at all times, now doubly so, hardly deserving the title of a meal, so poor and small were the portions of cornmeal, cooked in their frying-pans, which went for their rations, when the sound of artillery below broke on the quiet air. They were on their feet in an instant and at the guns, crowding upon the breastwork to look or to listen; for the road, as far as could be seen down the mountain, was empty except for their own picket, and lay as quiet as if sleeping in the balmy air. And yet volley after volley of artillery came rolling up the mountain. What could it mean? That the rest of their force had come up and was engaged with that at the foot of the mountain? The Colonel decided to be ready to go and help them; to fall on the enemy in the rear; perhaps they might capture the entire force. It seemed the natural thing to do, and the guns were limbered up in an incredibly short time, and a roadway made through the intrenchment, the men working like beavers under the excitement. Before they had left the redoubt, however, the vedettes sent out returned and reported that there was no engagement going on, and the firing below seemed to be only practising. There was quite a stir in the camp below; but they had not even broken camp. This was mysterious. Perhaps it meant that they had received reinforcements, but it was a queer way of showing it. The old Colonel sighed as he thought of the good ammunition they could throw away down there, and of his empty limber-chests. It was necessary to be on the alert, however; the guns were run back into their old places, and the horses picketed once more back among the trees. Meantime he sent another messenger back, this time a courier, for he had but one commissioned officer left, and the picket below was strengthened.

The morning passed and no one came; the day wore on and still no advance was made by the force below. It was suggested that the enemy had left; he had, at least, gotten enough of that battery. A reconnoissance, however, showed that he was still encamped at the foot

The Burial of the Guns

of the mountain. It was conjectured that he was trying to find a way around to take them in the rear, or to cross the ridge by the footpath. Preparation was made to guard more closely the mountain-path across the spur, and a detachment was sent up to strengthen the picket there. The waiting told on the men and they grew bored and restless. They gathered about the guns in groups and talked; talked of each piece some, but not with the old spirit and vim; the loneliness of the mountain seemed to oppress them; the mountains stretching up so brown and gray on one side of them, and so brown and gray on the other, with their bare, dark forests soughing from time to time as the wind swept up the pass. The minds of the men seemed to go back to the time when they were not so alone, but were part of a great and busy army, and some of them fell to talking of the past, and the battles they had figured in, and of the comrades they had lost. They told them off in a slow and colorless way, as if it were all part of the past as much as the dead they named. One hundred and nineteen times they had been in action. Only seventeen men were left of the eighty odd who had first enlisted in the battery, and of these four were at home crippled for life. Two of the oldest men had been among the half-dozen who had fallen in the skirmish just the day before. It looked tolerably hard to be killed that way after passing for four years through such battles as they had been in; and both had wives and children at home, too, and not a cent to leave them to their names. They agreed calmly that they'd have to "sort of look after them a little" if they ever got home. These were some of the things they talked about as they pulled their old worn coats about them, stuffed their thin, weather-stained hands in their ragged pockets to warm them, and squatted down under the breastwork to keep a little out of the wind. One thing they talked about a good deal was something to eat. They described meals they had had at one time or another as personal adventures, and discussed the chances of securing others in the future as if they were prizes of fortune. One listening and seeing their thin, worn faces and their wasted frames might have supposed they were starving, and they were, but they did not say so.

Towards the middle of the afternoon there was a sudden excitement in the camp. A dozen men saw them at the same time: a squad of three men down the road at the farthest turn,

The Burial of the Guns

past their picket; but an advancing column could not have created as much excitement, for the middle man carried a white flag. In a minute every man in the battery was on the breastwork. What could it mean! It was a long way off, nearly half a mile, and the flag was small: possibly only a pocket-handkerchief or a napkin; but it was held aloft as a flag unmistakably. A hundred conjectures were indulged in. Was it a summons to surrender? A request for an armistice for some purpose? Or was it a trick to ascertain their number and position? Some held one view, some another. Some extreme ones thought a shot ought to be fired over them to warn them not to come on; no flags of truce were wanted. The old Colonel, who had walked to the edge of the plateau outside the redoubt and taken his position where he could study the advancing figures with his field-glass, had not spoken. The lieutenant who was next in command to him had walked out after him, and stood near him, from time to time dropping a word or two of conjecture in a half-audible tone; but the Colonel had not answered a word; perhaps none was expected. Suddenly he took his glass down, and gave an order to the lieutenant: "Take two men and meet them at the turn yonder; learn their business; and act as your best judgment advises. If necessary to bring the messenger farther, bring only the officer who has the flag, and halt him at that rock yonder, where I will join him." The tone was as placid as if such an occurrence came every day. Two minutes later the lieutenant was on his way down the mountain and the Colonel had the men in ranks. His face was as grave and his manner as quiet as usual, neither more nor less so. The men were in a state of suppressed excitement. Having put them in charge of the second sergeant the Colonel returned to the breastwork. The two officers were slowly ascending the hill, side by side, the bearer of the flag, now easily distinguishable in his jaunty uniform as a captain of cavalry, talking, and the lieutenant in faded gray, faced with yet more faded red, walking beside him with a face white even at that distance, and lips shut as though they would never open again. They halted at the big bowlder which the Colonel had indicated, and the lieutenant, having saluted ceremoniously, turned to come up to the camp; the Colonel, however, went down to meet him. The two men met, but there was no spoken question; if the Colonel inquired it was only with the eyes. The lieutenant spoke, however. "He says," he began and stopped, then began again—"he says, General Lee—" again he choked, then blurted out, "I believe it is all a lie—a damned lie."

"Not dead? Not killed?" said the Colonel, quickly.

"No, not so bad as that; surrendered: surrendered his entire army at Appomattox day before yesterday. I believe it is all a damned lie," he broke out again, as if the hot denial relieved him. The Colonel simply turned away his face and stepped a pace or two off, and the two men stood motionless back to back for more than a minute. Then the Colonel stirred.

"Shall I go back with you?" the lieutenant asked, huskily.

The Colonel did not answer immediately. Then he said: "No, go back to camp and await my return." He said nothing about not speaking of the report. He knew it was not needed. Then he went down the hill slowly alone, while the lieutenant went up to the camp.

The interview between the two officers beside the bowlder was not a long one. It consisted of a brief statement by the Federal envoy of the fact of Lee's surrender two days before near Appomattox Court-House, with the sources of his information, coupled with a formal demand on the Colonel for his surrender. To this the Colonel replied that he had been detached and put under command of another officer for a specific purpose, and that his orders were to hold that pass, which he should do until he was instructed otherwise by his superior in command. With that they parted, ceremoniously, the Federal captain returning to where he had left his horse in charge of his companions a little below, and the old Colonel coming slowly up the hill to camp. The men were at once set to work to meet any attack which might be made. They knew that the message was of grave import, but not of how grave. They thought it meant that another attack would be made immediately, and they sprang to their work with renewed vigor, and a zeal as fresh as if it were but the beginning and not the end.

The time wore on, however, and there was no demonstration below, though hour after hour it was expected and even hoped for. Just as the sun sank into a bed of blue cloud a horseman was seen coming up the darkened mountain from the eastward side, and in a little while practised eyes reported him one of their own men—the sergeant who had been sent back the day before for ammunition. He was alone, and had something white before him on his horse—it could not be the ammunition; but perhaps that might be coming on behind. Every step of his jaded horse was anxiously watched. As he drew near, the lieutenant, after a word with the Colonel, walked down to meet him, and there was a short colloquy in the muddy road; then they came back together and slowly entered the camp, the sergeant handing down a bag of corn which he had got somewhere below, with the grim remark to his comrades, "There's your rations," and going at once to the Colonel's camp-fire, a little to one side among the trees, where the Colonel awaited him. A long conference was held, and then the sergeant left to take his luck with his mess, who were already parching the corn he had brought for their supper, while the lieutenant made the round of the camp; leaving the Colonel seated alone on a log by his camp-fire. He sat without moving, hardly stirring until the lieutenant returned from his round. A minute later the men were called from the guns and made to fall into line. They were silent, tremulous with suppressed excitement; the most sun-burned and weather-stained of them a little pale; the meanest, raggedest, and most insignificant not unimpressive in the deep and solemn silence with which they stood, their eyes fastened on the Colonel, waiting for him to speak. He stepped out in front of them, slowly ran his eye along the irregular line, up and down, taking in every man in his glance, resting on some longer than on others, the older men, then dropped them to the ground, and then suddenly, as if with an effort, began to speak. His voice had a somewhat metallic sound, as if it were restrained; but it was otherwise the ordinary tone of command. It was not much that he said: simply that it had become his duty to acquaint them with the information which he had received: that General Lee had surrendered two days before at Appomattox Court-House, yielding to overwhelming numbers; that this afternoon when he had first heard the report he had questioned its truth, but that it had been confirmed by one of their own men, and no longer admitted of doubt; that the rest of their own force, it was learned, had been captured, or had disbanded, and the enemy was now on both sides of the mountain; that a demand had been made on him that morning to surrender too; but that he had orders which he felt held good until

The Burial of the Guns

they were countermanded, and he had declined. Later intelligence satisfied him that to attempt to hold out further would be useless, and would involve needless waste of life; he had determined, therefore, not to attempt to hold their position longer; but to lead them out, if possible, so as to avoid being made prisoners and enable them to reach home sooner and aid their families. His orders were not to let his guns fall into the enemy's hands, and he should take the only step possible to prevent it. In fifty minutes he should call the battery into line once more, and roll the guns over the cliff into the river, and immediately afterwards, leaving the wagons there, he would try to lead them across the mountain, and as far as they could go in a body without being liable to capture, and then he should disband them, and his responsibility for them would end. As it was necessary to make some preparations he would now dismiss them to prepare any rations they might have and get ready to march.

All this was in the formal manner of a common order of the day; and the old Colonel had spoken in measured sentences, with little feeling in his voice. Not a man in the line had uttered a word after the first sound, half exclamation, half groan, which had burst from

The Burial of the Guns

them at the announcement of Lee's surrender. After that they had stood in their tracks like rooted trees, as motionless as those on the mountain behind them, their eyes fixed on their commander, and only the quick heaving up and down the dark line, as of horses overlaboring, told of the emotion which was shaking them. The Colonel, as he ended, half-turned to his subordinate officer at the end of the dim line, as though he were about to turn the company over to him to be dismissed; then faced the line again, and taking a step nearer, with a sudden movement of his hands towards the men as though he would have stretched them out to them, began again :

"Men," he said, and his voice changed at the word, and sounded like a father's or a brother's, "My men, I cannot let you go so. We were neighbors when the war began—many of us, and some not here to-night; we have been more since then—comrades, brothers in arms; we have all stood for one thing—for Virginia and the South; we have all done our duty—tried to do our duty; we have fought a good fight, and now it seems to be over, and we have been overwhelmed by numbers, not whipped—and we are going home. We have the future before us—we don't know just what

The Burial of the Guns

it will bring, but we can stand a good deal. We have proved it. Upon us depends the South in the future as in the past. You have done your duty in the past, you will not fail in the future. Go home and be honest, brave, self-sacrificing, God-fearing citizens, as you have been soldiers, and you need not fear for Virginia and the South. The war may be over; but you will ever be ready to serve your country. The end may not be as we wanted it, prayed for it, fought for it; but we can trust God; the end in the end will be the best that could be; even if the South is not free she will be better and stronger that she fought as she did. Go home and bring up your children to love her, and though you may have nothing else to leave them, you can leave them the heritage that they are sons of men who were in Lee's army."

He stopped, looked up and down the ranks again, which had instinctively crowded together and drawn around him in a half-circle; made a sign to the lieutenant to take charge, and turned abruptly on his heel to walk away. But as he did so, the long pent-up emotion burst forth. With a wild cheer the men seized him, crowding around and hugging him, as with protestations, prayers, sobs, oaths —

broken, incoherent, inarticulate — they swore to be faithful, to live loyal forever to the South, to him, to Lee. Many of them cried like children ; others offered to go down and have one more battle on the plain. The old Colonel soothed them, and quieted their excitement, and then gave a command about the preparations to be made. This called them to order at once ; and in a few minutes the camp was as orderly and quiet as usual : the fires were replenished ; the scanty stores were being overhauled ; the place was selected, and being got ready to roll the guns over the cliff ; the camp was being ransacked for such articles as could be carried, and all preparations were being hastily made for their march.

The old Colonel having completed his arrangements sat down by his camp-fire with paper and pencil, and began to write ; and as the men finished their work they gathered about in groups, at first around their camp-fires, but shortly strolled over to where the guns still stood at the breastwork, black and vague in the darkness. Soon they were all assembled about the guns. One after another they visited, closing around it and handling it from muzzle to trail as a man might a horse to try its sinew and bone, or a child to feel its fineness and warmth. They were for the most part silent, and when any sound came through the dusk from them to the officers at their fire, it was murmurous and fitful as of men speaking low and brokenly. There was no sound of the noisy controversy which was generally heard, the give-and-take of the camp-fire, the firing backwards and forwards that went on on the march; if a compliment was paid a gun by one of its special detachment, it was accepted by the others; in fact, those who had generally run it down now seemed most anxious to accord the piece praise. Presently a small number of the men returned to a camp-fire, and, building it up, seated themselves about it, gathering closer and closer together until they were in a little knot. One of them appeared to be writing, while two or three took up flaming chunks from the fire and held them as torches for him to see by. In time the entire company assembled about them, standing in respectful silence, broken only occasionally by a reply from one or another to some question from the scribe. After a little there was a sound of a roll-call, and reading and a short colloquy followed, and then two men, one with a paper in his hand, approached the fire beside which the officers sat still engaged.

"What is it, Harris?" said the Colonel to the man with the paper, who bore remnants of the chevrons of a sergeant on his stained and faded jacket.

"If you please, sir," he said, with a salute, "we have been talking it over, and we'd like this paper to go in along with that you're writing." He held it out to the lieutenant, who was the nearer and had reached forward to take it. "We s'pose you're agoin' to bury it with the guns," he said, hesitatingly, as he handed it over.

"What is it?" asked the Colonel, shading his eyes with his hands.

"It's just a little list we made out in and among us," he said, "with a few things we'd like to put in, so's if anyone ever hauls 'em out they'll find it there to tell what the old battery was, and if they don't, it'll be in one of 'em down thar 'til judgment, an' it'll sort of ease our minds a bit." He stopped and waited as a man who had delivered his message. The old Colonel had risen and taken the paper, and now held it with a firm grasp, as if it might blow away with the rising wind. He did not say a word, but his hand shook a little as he proceeded to fold it carefully, and there was a burning gleam in his deep-set eyes, back under his bushy, gray brows.

The Burial of the Guns

"Will you sort of look over it, sir, if you think it's worth while? We was in a sort of hurry and we had to put it down just as we come to it; we didn't have time to pick our ammunition; and it ain't written the best in the world, nohow." He waited again, and the Colonel opened the paper and glanced down at it mechanically. It contained first a roster, headed by the list of six guns, named by name: "Matthew," "Mark," "Luke," and "John," "The Eagle," and "The Cat"; then of the men, beginning with the heading:

"Those killed."

Then had followed "Those wounded," but this was marked out. Then came a roster of the company when it first entered service; then of those who had joined afterward; then of those who were present now. At the end of all there was this statement, not very well written, nor wholly accurately spelt:

"To Whom it may Concern: We, the above members of the old battery known, etc., of six guns, named, etc., commanded by the said Col. etc., left on the 11th day of April, 1865, have made out this roll of the battery, them as is gone and them as is left, to bury with the guns which the same we bury this night. We're all volunteers, every man; we joined the army at the beginning of the war, and we've stuck through to the end; sometimes we aint had much to eat, and sometimes we aint had nothin', but we've fought the best we could 119 battles and skirmishes as near as we can make out in four years, and never lost a gun. Now we're agoin' home. We aint surrendered; just disbanded, and we pledges ourselves to teach our children to love the South and General Lee; and to come when we're called anywheres an' anytime, so help us God."

There was a dead silence whilst the Colonel read.

"'Taint entirely accurite, sir, in one particular," said the sergeant, apologetically; "but we thought it would be playin' it sort o' low down on the Cat if we was to say we lost her unless we could tell about gittin' of her back, and the way she done since, and we didn't have time to do all that." He looked around as if to receive the corroboration of the other men, which they signified by nods and shuffling.

The Colonel said it was all right, and the paper should go into the guns.

"If you please, sir, the guns are all loaded,"

The Burial of the Guns

said the sergeant; "in and about our last charge, too; and we'd like to fire 'em off once more, jist for old times' sake to remember 'em by, if you don't think no harm could come of it?"

The Colonel reflected a moment and said it might be done; they might fire each gun separately as they rolled it over, or might get all ready and fire together, and then roll them over, whichever they wished. This was satisfactory.

The men were then ordered to prepare to march immediately, and withdrew for the purpose. The pickets were called in. In a short time they were ready, horses and all, just as they would have been to march ordinarily, except that the wagons and caissons were packed over in one corner by the camp with the harness hung on poles beside them, and the guns stood in their old places at the breastwork ready to defend the pass. The embers of the sinking camp-fires threw a faint light on them standing so still and silent. The old Colonel took his place, and at a command from him in a somewhat low voice, the men, except a detail left to hold the horses, moved into company-front facing the guns. Not a word was spoken, except the words of command. At the order each detachment went to its gun; the guns were run back and the men with their own hands ran them up on the edge of the perpendicular bluff above the river, where, sheer below, its waters washed its base, as if to face an enemy on the black mountain the other side. The pieces stood ranged in the order in which they had so often stood in battle, and the gray, thin fog rising slowly and silently from the river deep down between the cliffs, and wreathing the mountain-side above, might have been the smoke from some unearthly battle fought in the dim pass by ghostly guns, yet posted there in the darkness, manned by phantom gunners, while phantom horses stood behind, lit vaguely up by phantom camp-fires. At the given word the laniards were pulled together, and together as one the six black guns, belching flame and lead, roared their last challenge on the misty night, sending a deadly hail of shot and shell, tearing the trees and splintering the rocks of the farther side, and sending the thunder reverberating through the pass and down the mountain, startling from its slumber the sleeping camp on the hills below, and driving the browsing deer and the prowling mountain-fox in terror up the mountain.

There was silence among the men about the

The Burial of the Guns

guns for one brief instant and then such a cheer burst forth as had never broken from them even in battle: cheer on cheer, the long, wild, old familiar rebel yell for the guns they had fought with and loved.

The noise had not died away and the men behind were still trying to quiet the frightened horses when the sergeant, the same who had written, received from the hand of the Colonel a long package or roll which contained the records of the battery furnished by the men and by the Colonel himself, securely wrapped to make them water-tight, and it was rammed down the yet warm throat of the nearest gun: the Cat, and then the gun was tamped to the muzzle to make her water-tight, and, like her sisters, was spiked, and her vent tamped tight. All this took but a minute, and the next instant the guns were run up once more to the edge of the cliff; and the men stood by them with their hands still on them. A deadly silence fell on the men, and even the horses behind seemed to feel the spell. There was a long pause, in which not a breath was heard from any man, and the soughing of the tree-tops above and the rushing of the rapids below were the only sounds. They seemed to come from far, very far away. Then the Colonel said, quietly, "Let them go, and God be our helper, Amen." There was the noise in the darkness of trampling and scraping on the cliff-top for a second; the sound as of men straining hard together, and then with a pant it ceased all at once, and the men held their breath to hear. One second of utter silence; then one prolonged, deep, resounding splash sending up a great mass of white foam as the brass-pieces together plunged into the dark water below, and then the soughing of the trees and the murmur of the river came again with painful distinctness. It was full ten minutes before the Colonel spoke, though there were other sounds enough in the darkness, and some of the men, as the dark, outstretched bodies showed, were lying on the ground flat on their faces. Then the Colonel gave the command to fall in in the same quiet, grave tone he had used all night. The line fell in, the men getting to their horses and mounting in silence; the Colonel put himself at their head and gave the order of march, and the dark line turned in the darkness, crossed the little plateau between the smouldering campfires and the spectral caissons with the harness hanging beside them, and slowly entered the dim charcoal-burner's track. Not a word was spoken as they moved off. They might all have been phantoms. Only, the sergeant in the rear, as he crossed the little breastwork which ran along the upper side and marked the boundary of the little camp, half turned and glanced at the dying fires, the low, newly made mounds in the corner, the abandoned caissons, and the empty redoubt, and said, slowly, in a low voice to himself,

"Well, by God!"

The Gray Jacket of "No. 4"

THE GRAY JACKET OF "NO. 4"

MY meeting with him was accidental. I came across him passing through "the square." I had seen him once or twice on the street, each time lurching along so drunk that he could scarcely stagger, so that I was surprised to hear what he said about the war. He was talking to someone who evidently had been in the army himself, but on the other side—a gentleman with the loyal-legion button in his coat, and with a beautiful scar, a sabre-cut across his face. He was telling of a charge in some battle or skirmish in which, he declared, his company, not himself—for I remember he said he was "No. 4," and was generally told off to hold the horses; and that that day he had had the ill luck to lose his horse and get a little scratch himself, so he was not in the charge—did the finest work he ever saw, and really (so he claimed) saved the day. It was this self-abnegation that first arrested my attention, for I had been accustomed all my life to hear the war talked of; it was one of the inspiring influences in my humdrum existence. But the speakers, although they generally boasted of their commands, never of themselves individually, usually admitted that they themselves had been in the active force, and thus tacitly shared in the credit. "No. 4," however, expressly disclaimed that he was entitled to any of the praise, declaring that he was safe behind the crest of the hill (which he said he " hugged mighty close "), and claimed the glory for the rest of the command.

"It happened just as I have told you here," he said, in closing. "Old Joe saw the point as soon as the battery went to work, and sent Binford Terrell to the colonel to ask him to let him go over there and take it; and when Joe gave the word the boys went. They didn't go at a walk either, I tell you; it wasn't any promenade: they went clipping. At first the guns shot over 'em; didn't catch 'em till the third fire; then they played the devil with 'em : but the boys were up there right in 'em before they could do much. They turned the guns on 'em as they went down the hill (oh, our boys could handle the tubes then as well as the artillery themselves), and in a little while the rest of the line came up, and we formed a line of battle right there on that crest, and held it till nearly night. That's when I got jabbed. I picked up another horse, and with my foolishness went over there. That evening, you know, you all charged us—we were dismounted then. We lost more men then than we had done all day; there were forty-seven out of seventy-two killed or wounded. They walked all over us; two of 'em got hold of me (you see, I went to get our old flag some of you had got hold of). but I was too worthless to die. There were lots of 'em did go though, I tell you ; old Joe in the lead. Yes, sir ; the old company won that day, and old Joe led 'em. There ain't but a few of us left ; but when you want us, Colonel, you can get us. We'll stand by you."

He paused in deep reflection ; his mind evidently back with his old company and its gallant commander "old Joe," whoever he might be, who was remembered so long after he passed away in the wind and smoke of that unnamed evening battle. I took a good look at him—at "No. 4," as he called himself. He was tall, but stooped a little ; his features were good, at least his nose and brow were ; his mouth and chin were weak. His mouth was too stained with the tobacco which he chewed to tell much about it—and his chin was like so many American chins, not strong. His eyes looked weak. His clothes were very much worn, but they had once been good; they formerly had been black, and well made; the buttons were all on. His shirt was clean. I took note of this, for he had a dissipated look, and a rumpled shirt would have been natural. A man's linen tells on him before his other clothes. His listener had evidently been impressed by him also, for he arose, and said, abruptly, "Let's go and take a drink." To my surprise "No. 4" declined. "No, I thank you," he said, with promptness. I instinctively looked at him again to see if I had not misjudged him; but I concluded not, that I was right, and that he was simply "not drinking." I was flattered at my discrimination when I heard him say that he had "sworn off." His friend said no more, but remained standing while "No. 4" expatiated on the difference between a man who is drinking and one who is not. I never heard a more striking exposition of it. He said he wondered that any man could be such a fool as to drink liquor; that he had determined never to touch another drop. He presently relapsed into silence, and the other reached out his hand to say good-by. Suddenly rising, he said: "Well, suppose we go and have just one for old times' sake. Just one now, mind you; for I have not touched a drop in———." He turned away, and I did not catch the length of the time mentioned. But I have reason to believe that "No. 4" overstated it.

The next time I saw him was in the police court. I happened to be there when he walked out of the pen among as miscellaneous a lot of chronic drunkards, thieves, and miscreants of both sexes and several colors as were ever gathered together. He still had on his old black suit, buttoned up; but his linen was rumpled and soiled like himself, and he was manifestly just getting over a debauch, the effects of which were still visible on him in every line of his perspiring face and thin figure. He walked with that exaggerated erectness which told his self-deluded state as plainly as if he had pronounced it in words. He had evidently been there before, and more than once. The justice nodded to him familiarly:

"Here again?" he asked, in a tone part pleasantry, part regret.

"Yes, your honor. Met an old soldier last night, and took a drop for good fellowship, and before I knew it———" A shrug of the shoulders completed the sentence, and the shoulders did not straighten any more.

The tall officer who had picked him up said something to the justice in a tone too low for me to catch; but "No. 4" heard it—it was evidently a statement against him—for he started to speak in a deprecating way. The judge interrupted him:

"I thought you told me last time that if I let you go you would not take another drink for a year."

"I forgot," said "No. 4," in a low voice.

"This officer says you resisted him?"

The officer looked stolidly at the prisoner as if it were a matter of not the slightest interest to him personally. "Cursed me and abused me," he said, dropping the words slowly as if he were checking off a schedule.

"I did not, your honor; indeed, I did not," said "No. 4," quickly. "I swear I did not; he is mistaken. Your honor does not believe I would tell you a lie! Surely I have not got so low as that."

The justice turned his pencil in his hand doubtfully, and looked away. "No. 4" took in his position. He began again.

"I fell in with an old soldier, and we got to talking about the war—about old times." His voice was very soft. "I will promise your honor that I won't take another drink for a year.

Here, I'll take an oath to it. Swear me." He seized the greasy little Bible on the desk before him, and handed it to the justice. The magistrate took it doubtfully He looked down at the prisoner half kindly, half humorously.

"You'll just break it." He started to lay the book down.

"No; I want to take the pledge," said "No. 4," eagerly. "Did I ever break a pledge I made to your honor?"

"Didn't you promise me not to come back here?"

"I have not been here for nine months. Besides, I did not come of my own free will," said "No. 4," with a faint flicker of humor on his perspiring face.

"You were here two months ago, and you promised not to take another drink."

"I forgot that. I did not mean to break it; indeed, I did not. I fell in with——"

The justice looked away, considered a moment, and ordered him back into the pen with, "Ten days, to cool off."

"No. 4" stood quite still till the officer motioned him to the gate, behind which the prisoners sat in stolid rows. Then he walked dejectedly back into the pen, and sat down by another drunkard. His look touched me, and

I went around and talked to the magistrate privately. But he was inexorable; he said he knew more of him than I did, and that ten days in jail would "dry him out and be good for him." I told him the story of the battle. He knew it already, and said he knew more than that about him; that he had been one of the bravest soldiers in the whole army; did not know what fear was; had once ridden into the enemy and torn a captured standard from its captors' hands, receiving two desperate bayonet-wounds in doing it; and had done other acts of conspicuous gallantry on many occasions. I pleaded this, but he was obdurate; hard, I thought at the time, and told him so; told him he had been a soldier himself, and ought to be easier. He looked troubled, not offended; for we were friends, and I think he liked to see me, who had been a boy during the war, take up for an old soldier on that ground. But he stood firm. I must do him the justice to say that I now think it would not have made any difference if he had done otherwise. He had tried the other course many times.

"No. 4" must have heard me trying to help him, for one day, about a month after that, he walked in on me quite sober, and looking somewhat as he did the first day I saw him, thanked me for what I had done for him; delivered one of the most impressive discourses on intemperance that I ever heard; and asked me to try to help him get work. He was willing to do anything, he said; that is, anything he could do. I got him a place with a friend of mine which he kept a week, then got drunk. We got hold of him, however, and sobered him up, and he escaped the police and the justice's court. Being out of work, and very firm in his resolution never to drink again, we lent him some money — a very little — with which to keep along a few days, on which he got drunk immediately, and did fall into the hands of the police, and was sent to jail as before. This, in fact, was his regular round: into jail, out of jail; a little spell of sobriety, "an accidental fall," which occurred as soon as he could get a drop of liquor, and into jail again for thirty or sixty days, according to the degree of resistance he gave the police—who always, by their own account, simply tried to get him to go home, and, by his, insulted him—and to the violence of the language he applied to them. In this he excelled; for although as quiet as possible when he was sober, when he was drunk he was a terror, so the police said, and his resources of vituperation were cyclopedic. He possessed in this particular department an eloquence which was incredible. His blasphemy was vast, illimitable, infinite. He told me once that he could not explain it; that when he was sober he abhorred profanity, and never uttered an oath; when he was in liquor his brain took this turn, and distilled blasphemy in volumes. He said that all of its energies were quickened and concentrated in this direction, and then he took not only pleasure, but pride in it.

He told me a good deal of his life. He had got very low at this time, much lower than he had been when I first knew him. He recognized this himself, and used to analyze and discuss himself in quite an impersonal way. This was when he had come out of jail, and after having the liquor "dried out" of him. In such a state he always referred to his condition in the past as being something that never would or could recur; while on the other hand, if he were just over a drunk, he frankly admitted his absolute slavery to his habit. When he was getting drunk he shamelessly maintained, and was ready to swear on all the Bibles in creation, that he had not touched a drop, and never expected to do so again — indeed, could not be induced to do it—when in fact he would at the very time be reeking with the fumes of liquor, and perhaps had his pocket then bulging with a bottle which he had just emptied, and would willingly have bartered his soul to refill.

I never saw such absolute dominion as the love of liquor had over him. He was like a man in chains. He confessed it frankly and calmly. He said he had a disease, and gave me a history of it. It came on him, he said, in spells; that when he was over one he abhorred it, but when the fit seized him it came suddenly, and he was in absolute slavery to it. He said his father was a gentleman of convivial habits (I have heard that he was very dissipated, though not openly so, and "No. 4" never admitted it). He was killed at the battle of Bull Run. His mother—he always spoke of her with unvarying tenderness and reverence—had suffered enough, he said, to canonize her if she were not a saint already; she had brought him up to have a great horror of liquor, and he had never touched it till he went into the army. In the army he was in a convivial crowd, and they had hard marching and poor rations, often none. Liquor was scarce, and was regarded as a luxury; so although he was very much afraid of it, yet for good fellowship's sake, and because it was considered mannish, he used to drink it. Then he got to like it; and then got to feel the need of it, and took it to stimulate him when he was run down. This want brought with it a great depression when he did not have the means to satisfy it. He never liked the actual taste of it; he said few drunkards did. It was the effect that he was always after. This increased on him, he said, until finally it was no longer a desire, but a passion, a necessity; he was obliged to have it. He felt then that he would commit murder for it. "Why, I dream about it," he said. "I will tell you what I have done. I have made the most solemn vows, and have gone to bed and gone to sleep, and waked up and dressed and walked miles through the rain and snow to get it. I believe I would have done it if I had known I was going next moment to hell." He said it had ruined him; said so quite calmly; did not appear to have any special remorse about it; at least, never professed any; said it used to trouble him, but he had got over it now. He had had a plantation — that is, his mother had had—and he had been quite successful for a while; but he said, "A man can't drink liquor and run a farm," and the farm had gone.

I asked him how?

"I sold it," he said calmly; "that is, persuaded my mother to sell it. The stock that belonged to me had nearly all gone before. A man who is drinking will sell anything," he said. "I have sold everything in the world I had, or could lay my hands on. I have never got quite so low as to sell my old gray jacket that I used to wear when I rode behind old Joe. I mean to be buried in that—if I can keep it."

He had been engaged to a nice girl; the wedding-day had been fixed; but she had broken off the engagement. She married another man. "She was a mighty nice girl," he said, quietly. "Her people did not like my drinking so much. I passed her not long ago on the street. She did not know me." He glanced down at himself quietly. "She looks older than she did." He said that he had had a place for some time, did not drink a drop for nearly a year, and then got with some of the old fellows, and they persuaded him to take a little. "I cannot touch it. I have either got to drink or let it alone—one thing or the other," he said. "But I am all right now," he declared triumphantly, a little of the old fire lighting up in his face. "I never expect to touch a drop again."

He spoke so firmly that I was persuaded to make him a little loan, taking his due-bill for it, which he always insisted on giving. That evening I saw him being dragged along by three policemen, and he was cursing like a demon.

In the course of time he got so low that he spent much more than half his time in jail. He became a perfect vagabond, and with his clothes ragged and dirty might be seen reeling about or standing around the street corners near disreputable bars, waiting for a chance drink, or sitting asleep in doorways of untenanted buildings. His companions would be one or two chronic drunkards like himself, with red noses, bloated faces, dry hair, and filthy clothes. Sometimes I would see him hurrying along with one of these as if they had a piece of the most important business in the world. An idea had struck their addled brains that by some means they could manage to secure a drink. Yet in some way he still held himself above these creatures, and once or twice I heard of him being under arrest for resenting what he deemed an impertinence from them.

Once he came very near being drowned. There was a flood in the river, and a large crowd was watching it from the bridge. Suddenly a little girl's dog fell in. It was pushed in by a ruffian. The child cried out, and there was a commotion. When it subsided a man was seen swimming for life after the little white head going down the stream. It was "No. 4." He had slapped the fellow in the face, and then had sprung in after the dog. He caught it, and got out himself, though in too exhausted a state to stand up. When he was praised for it, he said, "A member of old Joe's company who would not have done that could not have ridden behind old Joe." I had this story from eye-witnesses, and it was used shortly after with good effect; for he was arrested for burglary, breaking into a man's house one night. It looked at first like a serious case, for some money had been taken out of a drawer; but when the case was investigated it turned out that the house was a bar-room over which the man lived,—he was the same man who had pitched the dog into the water,—and that "No. 4," after being given whiskey enough to make him a madman, had been put out of the place, had broken into the bar during the night to get more, and was found fast asleep in a chair with an empty bottle beside him. I think the jury became satisfied that if any money had been taken the barkeeper, to make out a case against "No. 4," had taken it himself. But there was a technical breaking, and it had to be got around; so his counsel appealed to the jury, telling them what he knew of "No. 4," together with the story of the child's dog, and "No. 4's" reply. There were one or two old soldiers on the jury, and they acquitted him, on which he somehow managed to get whiskey enough to land him back in jail in twenty-four hours.

In May, 1890, there was a monument unveiled in Richmond. It was a great occasion, and not only all Virginia, but the whole South, participated in it with great fervor, much enthusiasm, and many tears. It was an occasion for sacred memories. The newspapers talked about it for a good while beforehand; preparations were made for it as for the celebration of a great and general ceremony in which the whole South was interested. It was interested, because it was not only the unveiling of a monument for the old commander, the greatest and loftiest Southerner, and, as the South holds, man, of his time; it was an occasion consecrated to the whole South; it was the embalming in precious memories, and laying away in the tomb of the Southern Confederacy: the apotheosis of the Southern people. As such all were interested in it, and all prepared for it. It was known that all that remained of the Southern armies would be there: of the armies that fought at Shiloh, and Bull Run, and Fort

Republic; at Seven Pines, Gaines's Mill, and Cold Harbor; at Antietam, Fredericksburg, Chancellorsville, and Gettysburg; at Franklin, Atlanta, Murfreesboro, and Chickamauga, Spottsylvania, the Wilderness, and Petersburg; and the whole South, Union as it is now and ready to fight the nation's battles, gathered to glorify Lee, the old commander, and to see and glorify the survivors of those and other bloody fields in which the volunteer soldiers of the South had held the world at bay, and added to the glorious history of their race. Men came all the way from Oregon and California to be present. Old one-legged soldiers stumped it from West Virginia. Even "No. 4," though in the gutter, caught the contagion, and shaped up and became sober. He got a good suit of clothes somewhere—not new—and appeared quite respectable. He even got something to do, and, in token of what he had been, was put on one of the many committees having a hand in the entertainment arrangements. I never saw a greater change in anyone. It looked as if there was hope for him yet. He stopped me on the street a day or two before the unveiling and told me he had a piece of good news: the remnant of his old company was to be here; he had got hold of the last one,—there were nine of them left,—and he had his old jacket that he had worn in the war, and he was going to wear it on the march. "It's worn, of course," he said, "but my mother put some patches over the holes, and except for the stain on it it's in good order. I believe I am the only one of the boys that has his jacket still; my mother kept this for me; I have never got so hard up as to part with it. I'm all right now. I mean to be buried in it."

I had never remarked before what a refined face he had; his enthusiasm made him look younger than I had ever seen him.

I saw him on the day before the eve of the unveiling; he was as busy as a bee, and looked almost handsome. "The boys are coming in by every train," he said. "Look here." He pulled me aside, and unbuttoned his vest. A piece of faded gray cloth was disclosed. He had the old gray jacket on under his other coat. "I know the boys will like to see it," he said. "I'm going down to the train now to meet one—Binford Terrell. I don't know whether I shall know him. Binford and I used to be much of a size. We did not use to speak at one time; had a falling out about which one should hold the horses; I made him do it, but I reckon he won't remember it now. I don't.

I have not touched a drop. Good-by." He went off.

The next night about bedtime I got a message that a man wanted to see me at the jail immediately. It was urgent. Would I come down there at once? I had a foreboding, and I went down. It was as I suspected. "No. 4" was there behind the bars. "Drunk again," said the turnkey, laconically, as he let me in. He let me see him. He wanted me to see the judge and get him out. He besought me. He wept. "It was all an accident;" he had "found some of the old boys, and they had got to talking over old times, and just for old times' sake," etc. He was too drunk to stand up; but the terror of being locked up next day had sobered him, and his mind was perfectly clear. He implored me to see the judge and to get him to let him out. "Tell him I will come back here and stay a year if he will let me out to-morrow," he said brokenly. He showed me the gray jacket under his vest, and was speechless. Even then he did not ask release on the ground that he was a veteran. I never knew him to urge this reason. Even the officials who must have seen him there fifty times were sympathetic; and they told me to see the justice, and they believed he would let him out for next day. I applied to him as they suggested. He said, "Come down to court to-morrow morning." I did so. "No. 4" was present, pale and trembling. As he stood there he made a better defence than any one else could have made for him. He admitted his guilt, and said he had nothing to say in extenuation except that it was the "old story," he "had not intended it; he deserved it all, but would like to get off that day; had a special reason for it, and would, if necessary, go back to jail that evening and stay there a year, or all his life." As he stood awaiting sentence, he looked like a damned soul. His coat was unbuttoned, and his old, faded gray jacket showed under it. The justice, to his honor, let him off: let all offenders off that day. "No. 4" shook hands with him, unable to speak, and turned away. Then he had a strange turn. We had hard work to get him to go into the procession. He positively refused; said he was not fit to go, or to live; began to cry, and took off his jacket. He would go back to jail, he said. We finally got him straight; accepted from him a solemn promise not to touch a drop till the celebration was over, so help him God, and sent him off to join his old command at the tobacco-warehouse on the slip where the cavalry rendezvoused. I had some apprehension that he would not turn up in the procession; but I was mistaken. He was there with the old cavalry veterans, as sober as a judge, and looking every inch a soldier.

It was a strange scene, and an impressive one even to those whose hearts were not in sympathy with it in any respect. Many who had been the hardest fighters against the South were in sympathy with much of it, if not with all. But to those who were of the South, it was sublime. It passed beyond mere enthusiasm, however exalted, and rested in the profoundest and most sacred deeps of their being. There were many cheers, but more tears; not tears of regret or mortification, but tears of sympathy and hallowed memory. The gayly decorated streets, in all the bravery of fluttering ensigns and bunting; the martial music of many bands; the constant tramp of marching troops; the thronged sidewalks, verandas, and roofs; the gleam of polished arms and glittering uniforms; the flutter of gay garments, and the smiles of beautiful women sweet with sympathy; the long line of old soldiers, faded and broken and gray, yet each self-sustained, and inspired by the life of the South that flowed in their veins, marching under the old Confederate battle-flags that they had borne so often in victory and in defeat

—all contributed to make the outward pageant a scene never to be forgotten. But this was merely the outward image; the real fact was the spirit. It was the South. It was the spirit of the South; not of the new South, nor yet merely of the old South, but the spirit of the great South. When the young troops from every Southern State marched by in their fresh uniforms, with well-drilled battalions, there were huzzas, much applause and enthusiasm; when the old soldiers came there was a tempest: wild cheers choking with sobs and tears, the well-known, once-heard-never-forgotten cry of the battling South, known in history as "the rebel yell." Men and women and children joined in it. It began at the first sight of the regular column, swelled up the crowded streets, rose to the thronged housetops, ran along them for squares like a conflagration, and then came rolling back in volume only to rise and swell again greater than before. Men wept; children shrilled; women sobbed aloud. What was it! Only a thousand or two of old or aging men riding or tramping along through the dust of the street, under some old flags, dirty and ragged and stained. But they represented the spirit of the South; they represented the spirit which when honor was in question never counted the cost; the spirit that had stood up for the South against overwhelming odds for four years, and until the South had crumbled and perished under the forces of war; the spirit that is the strongest guaranty to us to-day that the Union is and is to be; the spirit that, glorious in victory, had displayed a fortitude yet greater in defeat. They saw in every stain on those tattered standards the blood of their noblest, bravest, and best; in every rent a proof of their glorious courage and sacrifice. They saw in those gray and careworn faces, in those old clothes interspersed now and then with a faded gray uniform, the men who in the ardor of their youth had, for the South, faced death undaunted on a hundred fields, and had never even thought it great; men who had looked immortality in the eyes, yet had been thrown down and trampled underfoot, and who were greater in their overthrow than when glory poured her light upon their upturned faces. Not one of them all but was self-sustaining, sustained by the South, or had ever even for one moment thought in his direst extremity that he would have what was, undone.

The crowd was immense; the people on the fashionable street up which the procession passed were fortunate: they had the advantage of their yards and porticos, and they threw them open to the public. Still the throng on the sidewalks was tremendous, and just before the old veterans came along the crush increased. As it resettled itself I became conscious that a little old woman in a rusty black dress whom I had seen patiently standing alone in the front line on the street corner for an hour had lost her position, and had been pushed back against the railing, and had an anxious, disappointed look on her face. She had a little, faded knot of Confederate colors fastened in her old dress, and, almost hidden by the crowd, she was looking up and down in some distress to see if she could not again get a place from which she could see. Finally she seemed to give it up, and stood quite still, tiptoeing now and then to try to catch a glimpse. I saw someone about to help her when, from a gay and crowded portico above her, a young and beautiful girl in a white dress, whom I had been observing for some time as the life of a gay party, as she sat in her loveliness, a queen on her throne with her courtiers around her, suddenly arose and ran down into the street. There was a short colloquy. The young beauty was offering something which the old lady was declining; but it ended in the young girl leading the older woman gently up on to her veranda and giving her the chair of state. She was hardly seated when the old soldiers began to pass.

As the last mounted veterans came by, I remembered that I had not seen "No. 4;" but as I looked up, he was just coming along. In his hand, with staff resting on his toe, he carried an old standard so torn and tattered and stained that it was scarcely recognizable as a flag. I did not for a moment take in that it was he, for he was not in the gray jacket which I had expected to see. He was busy looking down at the throng on the sidewalk, apparently searching for some one whom he expected to find there. He was in some perplexity, and pulled in his horse, which began to rear. Suddenly the applause from the portico above arrested his attention, and he looked toward it and bowed. As he did so his eye caught that of the old lady seated there. His face lighted up, and, wheeling his prancing horse half around, he dipped the tattered standard, and gave the royal salute as though saluting a queen. The old lady pressed her wrinkled hand over the knot of faded ribbon on her breast, and made a gesture to him, and he rode on. He had suddenly grown handsome. I looked at her again; her eyes were closed, her hands were clasped, and her lips were moving.

I saw the likeness: she was his mother. As he passed me I caught his eye. He saw my perplexity about the jacket, glanced up at the torn colors, and pointed to a figure just beyond him dressed in a short, faded jacket. "No. 4" had been selected, as the highest honor, to carry the old colors which he had once saved; and not to bear off all the honors from his friend, he had with true comradeship made Binford Terrell wear his cherished jacket. He made a brave figure as he rode away, and my cheer died on my lips as I thought of the sad, old mother in her faded knot, and of the dashing young soldier who had saved the colors in that unnamed fight.

After that we got him a place, and he did well for several months. He seemed to be cured. New life and strength appeared to come back to him. But his mother died, and one night shortly afterward he disappeared, and remained lost for several days. When we found him he had been brought to jail, and I was sent for to see about him. He was worse than I had ever known him. He was half-naked and little better than a madman. I went to a doctor about him, an old army surgeon, who saw him, and shook his head. "*Mania a potu.* Very bad; only a question of time," he said. This was true. "No. 4" was beyond hope.

Body and brain were both gone. It got to be only a question of days, if not of hours. Some of his other friends and I determined that he should not die in jail; so we took him out and carried him to a cool, pleasant room looking out on an old garden with trees in it. There in the dreadful terror of raving delirium he passed that night. I with several others sat up with him. I could not have stood many more like it. All night long he raved and tore. His oaths were blood-curdling. He covered every past portion of his life. His army life was mainly in his mind. He fought the whole war over. Sometimes he prayed fervently; prayed against his infirmity; prayed that his chains might be broken. Then he would grow calm for awhile. One thing recurred constantly: he had sold his honor, betrayed his cause. This was the order again and again, and each time the paroxysm of frightful fury came on, and it took all of us to hold him. He was covered with snakes: they were chains on his wrists and around his body. He tried to pull them from around him. At last, toward morning, came one of those fearful spells, worse than any that had gone before. It passed, and he suddenly seemed to collapse. He sank, and the stimulant administered failed to revive him.

"He is going," said the doctor, quietly, across the bed. Whether his dull ear caught the word or not, I cannot say; but he suddenly roused up, tossed one arm, and said:

"Binford, take the horses. I'm going to old Joe," and sank back.

"He's gone," said the doctor, opening his shirt and placing his ear over his heart. As he rose up I saw two curious scars on "No. 4's" emaciated breast. They looked almost like small crosses, about the size of the decorations the European veterans wear. The old doctor bent over and examined them.

"Hello! Bayonet-wounds," he said briefly.

A little later I went out to get a breath of fresh morning air to quiet my nerves, which were somewhat unstrung. As I passed by a little second-hand clothing-store of the meanest kind, in a poor, back street, I saw hanging up outside an old gray jacket. I stopped to examine it. It was stained behind with mud, and in front with a darker color. An old patch hid a part of the front; but a close examination showed two holes over the breast. It was "No. 4's" lost jacket. I asked the shopman about it. He had bought it, he said, of a pawnbroker who had got it from some drunkard, who had probably stolen it last year from some old soldier. He readily sold it, and I took it back with me; and the others being gone, an old woman and I cut the patch off it and put "No. 4's" stiffening arms into the sleeves. Word was sent to us during the day to say that the city would bury him in the poorhouse grounds. But we told them that arrangements had been made; that he would have a soldier's burial. And he had it.

Miss Dangerlie's Roses

MISS DANGERLIE'S ROSES

HENRY FLOYD was a crank, at least so many people said; a few thought he was a wonderful person: these were mostly children, old women, and people not in the directory, and persons not in the directory do not count for much. He was in fact a singular fellow. It was all natural enough to him; he was just like what he believed his father had been, his father of whom his mother used to tell him, and whom he remembered so vaguely except when he had suddenly loomed up in his uniform at the head of his company, when they went away on that march from which he had never returned. He meant to be like him, if he was not, and he remembered all that his mother had told him of his gentleness, his high courtesy, his faithfulness, his devotion to duty, his unselfishness. So it was all natural enough to Floyd to be as he was. But a man can no more tell whether or not he is a crank than he can tell how old he looks. He was, however, without doubt, different in certain ways from most people. This his friends admitted. Some said he was old-fashioned; some that he was "old-timey;" some that he was unpractical, the shades of criticism ranging up to those saying he was a fool. This did not mean intellectually, for none denied his intellect. He drove a virile pen, and had an epigrammatic tongue. He had had a hard time. He had borne the yoke in his youth. This, we have strong authority for saying, is good for a man; but it leaves its mark upon him. He had been desperately poor. He had not minded that except for his mother, and he had approved of her giving up every cent to meet the old security debts. It had cut him off from his college education; but he had worked till he was a better scholar than he might have been had he gone to college. He had kept his mother comfortable as long as she lived, and then had put up a monument over her in the old churchyard, as he had done before to his father's memory. This, everyone said, was foolish, and perhaps it was, for it took him at least two years to pay for them, and he might have laid up the money and got a start, or, as some charitable persons said, it might have been given to the poor. However, the monuments were put up, and on them were epitaphs which recorded at length the virtues of those to whom they were erected, with their descent, and declared that they were Christians and Gentlepeople. Some one said to Floyd that he might have shortened the epitaphs, and have saved something. "I did not want them shortened," said he.

He had borne the yoke otherwise also. One of the first things he had done after starting in life was to fall in love with a beautiful woman. She was very beautiful and a great belle. Every one said it was sheer nonsense for Henry Floyd to expect her to marry him, as poor as he was, which was natural enough. The only thing was that she led Floyd to believe she was going to marry him when she did not intend to do it, and it cost him a great deal of unhappiness. He never said one word against her, not even when she married a man much older than himself, simply, as everyone said, because he was very rich. If Floyd ever thought that she treated him badly, no one ever knew it, and when finally she left her husband, no one ever ventured to discuss it before Floyd.

Henry Floyd, however, had suffered,—that everyone could see who had eyes; but only he knew how much. Generally grave and dreamy;

when quiet as calm as a dove, as fierce as a hawk when aroused; moving always in an eccentric orbit, which few understood; flashing out now and then gleams which some said were sparks of genius but which most people said were mere eccentricity, he had sunk into a recluse. He was in this state when he met HER. He always afterward referred to her so. He was at a reception when he came upon her on a stairway. A casual word about his life, a smile flashed from her large, dark, luminous eyes, lighting up her face, and Henry Floyd awoke. She had called him from the dead. It was a case of love at first sight. From that time he never had a thought for anyone else, least of all for himself. He lived in her and for her. He blossomed under her sympathy as a tree comes out under the sunshine and soft breath of spring. He grew, he broadened. She was his sun, his breath of life; he worshipped her. Then one day she died—suddenly—sank down and died as a butterfly might die, chilled by a blast. With her Henry Floyd buried his youth. For a time people were sympathetic; but they began immediately to speculate about him, then to gossip about him. It made no difference to him or in him. He was like a man that is dead, who felt no more. One thing about a great sorrow is that it destroys all lesser ones. A man with a crushed body does not feel pinpricks. Henry Floyd went on his way calmly, doggedly, mechanically. He drifted on and was talked about continually. Gossip would not let him alone, so she did him the honor to connect his name with that of every woman he met. In fact, there was as much reason to mention all as one. He was fond of women, and enjoyed them. Women liked him too. There was a certain gentleness mingled with firmness, a kind of protecting air about him which women admired, and a mystery of impenetrable sadness which women liked. Every woman who knew him trusted him, and had a right to trust him. To none was he indifferent, but in none was he interested. He was simply cut off. A physician who saw him said, " That man is dying of loneliness." This went on for some years. At last his friends determined to get him back into society. They made plans for him and carried them out to a certain length; there the plans failed. Floyd might be led up to the water, but none could make him drink; there he took the bit in his teeth and went his own way. He would be invited to meet a girl at a dinner got up for his benefit, that he might meet her, and would spend the

Miss Dangerlie's Roses

evening hanging over a little unheard-of country cousin with a low voice and soft eyes, entertaining her with stories of his country days or of his wanderings; or he would be put by some belle, and after five minutes' homage spend the time talking to some old lady about her grandchildren. "You must marry," they said to him. "When one rises from the dead," he replied. At length, his friends grew tired of helping him and gave him up, and he dropped out and settled down. Commiseration is one of the bitter things of life. But Floyd had what is harder to bear than that. It did not affect his work. It was only his health and his life that suffered. He was like a man who has lost the senses of touch and taste and sight. If he minded it, he did not show it. One can get used to being bedridden.

One thing about him was that he always appeared poor. He began to be known as an inventor and writer. It was known that he received high prices for what he did; but he appeared to be no better off than when he made nothing. Some persons supposed that he gambled; others whispered that he spent it in other dissipation. In fact, one lady gave a circumstantial account of the way he squandered his money, and declared herself very glad that he had never visited her daughters. When this was repeated to Floyd, he said he fortunately did not have to account to her for the way he spent his money. He felt that the woman out under the marble cross knew how his money went, and so did the little cousin who was named after her, and who was at school. He had a letter from her in his pocket at that moment. So he drifted on.

At length one evening he was at a reception in a strange city whither his business had taken him. The rooms were filled with light and beauty. Floyd was standing chatting with a child of ten years, whom he found standing in a corner, gazing out with wide questioning eyes on the throng. They were friends instantly, and he was telling her who the guests were, as they came sailing in, giving them fictitious names and titles. "They are all queens," he told her, at which she laughed. She pointed out a tall and stately woman with a solemn face, and with a gleaming bodice on like a cuirass, and her hair up on her head like a casque. "Who is that?"

"Queen Semiramis."

"And who is that?" It was a stout lady with a tiara of diamonds, a red face, and three feathers.

"Queen Victoria, of course."

"And who am I?" She placed her little hand on her breast with a pretty gesture.

"The Queen of Hearts," said Floyd, quickly, at which she laughed outright. "Oh! I must not laugh," she said, checking herself and glancing around her with a shocked look. "I forgot."

"You shall. If you don't, you sha'n't know who another queen is."

"No, mamma told me I must not make a bit of noise; it is not style, you know, but you mustn't be so funny."

"Good heavens!" said Floyd.

"Oh! who is this coming?" A lady richly dressed was making her way toward them. "The Queen of Sheba—coming to see Solomon," said Floyd, as she came up to him. "Let me introduce you to a beautiful girl, Sarah Dangerlie," she said, and drew him through the throng toward a door, where he was presented to a tall and strikingly handsome girl and made his bow and a civil speech, to which the young lady responded with one equally polite and important. Other men were pressing around her, to all of whom she made apt and cordial speeches, and Floyd fell back and rejoined his little girl, whose face lit up at his return.

"Oh! I was so afraid you were going away with her."

"And leave you? Never, I'm not so easily disposed of."

"Everyone goes with her. They call her the Queen."

"Do they?"

"Do you like her?"

"Yes."

"You don't," she said, looking at him keenly.

"Yes, she is beautiful."

"Everyone says so."

"She isn't as beautiful as someone else I know," said Floyd, pleasantly.

"Isn't she? As whom?"

Floyd took hold of the child's hand and said, "Let's go and get some supper."

"I don't like her," said the little girl, positively.

"Don't you?" said Floyd. He stopped and glanced across the room toward where the girl had stood. He saw only the gleam of her fine shoulders as she disappeared in the crowd surrounded by her admirers.

A little later Floyd met the young lady on the stairway. He had not recognized her, and was passing on, when she spoke to him.

"I saw you talking to a little friend of mine," she began, then—"Over in the corner," she explained.

"Oh! yes. She is sweet. They interest me. I always feel when I have talked with a child as if I had got as near to the angels as one can get on earth."

"Do you know I was very anxious to meet you," she said.

"Were you? Thank you. Why?"

"Because of a line of yours I once read."

"I am pleased to have written only one line that attracted your attention," said Floyd, bowing.

"No, no—it was this—

"'The whitest soul of man or saint is black beside a girl's.'"

"Beside a child's," said Floyd, correcting her.

"Oh! yes, so it is—'beside a child's.'"

Her voice was low and musical. Floyd glanced up and caught her look, and the color deepened in her cheek as the young man suddenly leant a little towards her and gazed earnestly into her eyes, which she dropped, but instantly raised again.

"Yes—good-night," she held out her hand, with a taking gesture and smile.

"Good-night," said Floyd, and passed on up the stairs to the dressing-room. He got his coat and hat and came down the stairway. A group seized him.

"Come to the club," they said. He declined.

"Roast oysters and beer," they said.

"No, I'm going home."

"Are you ill?" asked a friend.

"No, not at all. Why?"

"You look like a man who has seen a spirit."

"Do I? I'm tired, I suppose. Good-night,—good-night, gentlemen," and he passed out.

"Perhaps I have," he said as he went down the cold steps into the frozen street.

Floyd went home and tossed about all night. His life was breaking up, he was all at sea. Why had he met her? He was losing the anchor that had held him. "They call her the queen," the little girl had said. She must be. He had seen her soul through her eyes.

Floyd sent her the poem which contained the line which she had quoted; and she wrote him a note thanking him. It pleased him. It was sympathetic. She invited him to call. He went to see her. She was fine in grain and in look. A closely fitting dark gown ornamented by a single glorious red rose which might have grown where it lay, and her soft hair coiled on her small head, as she entered tall and straight and calm, made Floyd involuntarily say to himself, " Yes "—

" She was right," he said, half to himself, half aloud, as he stood gazing at her with inquiring eyes after she had greeted him cordially.

" What was right ? " she asked.

" Something a little girl said about you."

" What was it ? "

" I will tell you some day, when I know you better."

" Was it a compliment ? "

" Yes."

" Tell me now."

" No, wait."

He came to know her better; to know her very well. He did not see her very often, but he thought of her a great deal. He seemed to find in her a sympathy which he needed. It reminded him of the past. He awoke from his lethargy; began to work once more in the old way; mixed among men again; grew brighter. "Henry Floyd is growing younger, instead of older," someone said of him. " His health has been bad," said a doctor. "He is improving. I thought at one time he was going to die." "He is getting rich," said a broker, who had been a schoolmate of his. "I see he has just invented a new something or other to relieve children with hip or ankle-joint disease."

"Yes, and it is a capital thing, too ; it is being taken up by the profession. I use it. It is a curious thing that he should have hit on that when he is not a surgeon. He had studied anatomy as a sort of fad, as he does everything. One of Haile Tabb's boys was bedridden, and he was a great friend of his, and that set him at it."

"I don't think he's so much of a crank as he used to be," said someone.

The broker who had been his schoolmate met Floyd next day.

"I see you have been having a great stroke of luck," he said.

"Have I?"

"Yes. I see in the papers, that your discovery, or invention, or whatever it was, has been taken up."

"Oh! yes—that? It has."

"I congratulate you."

"Thank you."

"I would not mind looking into that."

"Yes, it is interesting."

"I might take an interest in it."

"Yes, I should think so."

"How much do you ask for it?"

"'Ask for it?' Ask for what?"

"For an interest in it, either a part or the whole?"

"What?"

"You ought to make a good thing out of it—out of your patent."

"My patent! I haven't any patent."

"What! No patent?"

"No. It's for the good of people generally."

"But you got a patent?"

"No."

"Couldn't you get a patent?"

"I don't know."

"Well, I'll be bound I'd have got a patent."

"Oh! no, I don't think so."

"I tell you what, you ought to turn your talents to account," said his friend.

"Yes, I know I ought."

"You could be a rich man."

"But I don't care to be rich."

"What! Oh! nonsense. Everyone does."

"I do not. I want to live."

"But you don't live."

"Well, maybe I shall some day."

"You merely exist."

"Why should I want to be rich?"

"To live—to buy what you want."

"I want sympathy, love; can one buy that?"

"Yes—even that."

"No, you cannot. There is only one sort of woman to be bought."

"Well, come and see me sometimes, won't you?"

"Well, no, I'm very much obliged to you; but I don't think I can."

"Why? I have lots of rich men come to my house. You'd find it to your advantage if you'd come."

"Thank you."

"We could make big money together if——"

He paused. Floyd was looking at him.

"Could we? If—what?"

"If you would let me use you."

"Thank you," said Floyd. "Perhaps we could."

"Why won't you come?"

"Well, the fact is, I haven't time. I shall

have to wait to get a little richer before I can afford it. Besides I have a standing engagement."

"Oh! no, we won't squeeze you. I tell you what, come up to dinner to-morrow. I'm going to have a fellow there, an awfully rich fellow—want to interest him in some things, and I've invited him down. He is young Router, the son of the great Router, you know who he is?"

"Well, no, I don't believe I do. Good-by. Sorry I can't come; but I have an engagement."

"What is it?"

"To play mumble-the-peg with some boys: Haile Tabb's boys."

"Oh! hang the boys! Come up to dinner. It is an opportunity you may not have again shortly. Router's awfully successful, and you can interest him. I tell you what I'll do——"

"No, thank you, I'll keep my engagement. Good-by."

"That fellow's either a fool or he is crazy," said his friend, gazing after him as he walked away. "And he's got some sense too. If he'd let me use him I could make money out of him for both of us."

It was not long before Floyd began to be

known more widely. He had schemes for the amelioration of the condition of the poor. They were pronounced quixotic; but he kept on. He said he got good out of them if no one else did.

He began to go oftener and oftener down to the City, where Miss Dangerlie lived. He did not see a great deal of her; but he wrote to her. He found in her a ready sympathy with his plans. It was not just as it used to be in his earlier love affair, where he used to find himself uplifted and borne along by the strong spirit which had called him from the dead; but if it was not this that he got, it was what contented him. Whatever he suggested, she accepted. He found in her tastes a wonderful similarity with his, and from that he drew strength.

Women in talking of him in connection with her said it was a pity; men said he was lucky.

One evening, at a reception at her house, he was in the gentlemen's dressing-room. It was evidently a lady's apartment which had been devoted for the occasion as a dressing-room. It was quite full at the time. A man, a large fellow with sleek, short hair, a fat chin, and a dazzling waistcoat, pulled open a lower drawer in a bureau. Articles of a lady's apparel

were discovered, spotless and neatly arranged.
"Shut that drawer instantly," said Floyd, in a low, imperious tone.

"Suppose I don't, what then?"

"I will pitch you out of that window," said Floyd, quietly, moving a step nearer to him. The drawer was closed, and the man turned away.

"Do you know who that was?" asked someone of Floyd.

"No, not the slightest idea."

"That was young Router, the son of the great Router."

"Who is the-great-Router?"

"The great pork man. His son is the one who is so attentive to Miss Dangerlie."

"I am glad he closed the drawer," said Floyd, quietly.

"He is said to be engaged to her," said the gentleman.

"He is not engaged to her," said Floyd.

Later on he was talking to Miss Dangerlie. He had taken her out of the throng. "Do you know who introduced me to you?" he asked.

"Yes, Mrs. Drivington."

"No, a little girl."

"Who? Why, don't you remember! I am surprised. It was just in the doorway!"

"Oh! yes, I remember well enough. I met a beauty there, but I did not care for her. I met you first on the stairway, and a child introduced me."

"Children interest me, they always admire one," she said.

"They interest me, I always admire them," he said. "They are true."

She was silent, then changed the subject.

"A singular little incident befell me this evening," she said. "As I was coming home from a luncheon-party, a wretched woman stopped me and asked me to let her look at me."

"You did it, of course," he said.

She looked at him with her eyes wide open with surprise.

"What do you suppose a man said to me upstairs?" he asked her.

"What?"

"That you were engaged to someone."

"What! That I was engaged! To whom, pray?" She looked incredulous.

"To a fellow I saw up there—Mr. 'Router,' I think he said was his name."

"The idea! Engaged to Mr. Router! You did not believe him, did you?"

"No, of course I did not; I trust you entirely."

She buried her face in the roses she held in her hand, and did not speak. Her other hand rested on the arm of her chair next him. It was fine and white. He laid his on it firmly, and leaning towards her, said, "I beg your pardon for mentioning it. I am not surprised that you are hurt. Forgive me. I could not care for you so much if I did not believe in you."

"It was so kind in you to send me these roses," she said. "Aren't they beautiful?"

She turned them round and gazed at them with her face slightly averted.

"Yes, they are, and yet I hate to see them tied that way; I ordered them sent to you loose. I always like to think of you as arranging roses."

"Yes, I love to arrange them myself," she said.

"The fact is, as beautiful as those are, I believe I like better the old-fashioned roses right out of the dew. I suppose it is old association. But I know an old garden up at an old country-place, where my mother used to live as a girl. It used to be filled up with roses, and I always think of the roses there as sweeter than any others in the world."

"Yes, I like the old-fashioned roses best

too," she said, with that similarity of taste which always pleased him."

"The next time I come to see you I am going to bring you some of those roses," he said. "My mother used to tell me of my father going out and getting them for her, and I would like you to have some of them."

"Oh! thank you. How far is it from your home?"

"Fifteen or twenty miles."

"But you cannot get them there."

"Oh! yes, I can; the fact is, I own the place." She looked interested. "Oh! it is not worth anything as land," he said, "but I love the association. My mother was brought up there, and I keep up the garden just as it was. You shall have the roses. Some day I want to see you among them." Just then there was a step behind him. She rose.

"Is it ours?" she asked someone over her shoulder.

"Yes, come along."

Floyd glanced around. It was the "son of the great Router."

She turned to Floyd, and said, in an earnest undertone, "I am very sorry; but I had an engagement. Good-by." She held out her hand. Floyd took it and pressed it.

"Good-by," he said, tenderly. "That is all right."

She took the-son-of-the-great-Router's arm.

. . . .

One afternoon, a month after Miss Dangerlie's reception, Henry Floyd was packing his trunk. He had just looked at his watch, when there was a ring at the bell. He knew it was the postman, and a soft look came over his face as he reflected that even if he got no letter he would see her within a few hours. A large box of glorious old-fashioned roses was on the floor near him, and a roll of money and a time-table lay beside it. He had ridden thirty miles that morning to get and bring the roses himself for one whom he always thought of in connection with them.

A letter was brought in, and a pleased smile lit up the young man's face as he saw the handwriting. He laid on the side of the trunk a coat that he held, and then sat down on the arm of a chair and opened the letter. His hand stroked it softly as if it were of velvet. He wore a pleased smile as he began to read. Then the smile died away and a startled look took its place. The color faded out of his face, and his mouth closed firmly. When he was through he turned back and read the letter all

Miss Dangerlie's Roses

over again, slowly. It seemed hard to understand; for after a pause he read it over a third time. Then he looked straight before him for a moment, and then slowly tore it up into thin shreds and crumpled them up in his hand. Ten minutes later he rose from his seat and dropped the torn pieces into the fireplace. He walked over and put on his hat and coat, and going out, pulled the door firmly to behind him. The trunk, partly packed, stood open with the half-folded coat hanging over its edge and with the roses lying by its side.

Floyd walked into the Club and, returning quietly the salutations of a group of friends, went over to a rack and drew out a newspaper file, with which he passed into another room.

"Announcement of Engagement: Router and Dangerlie," was the heading on which his eye rested. "It is stated," ran the paragraph, "that they have been engaged some time, but no announcement has been made until now, on the eve of the wedding, owing to the young lady's delicacy of feeling."

That night Henry Floyd wrote a letter. This was the close of it:

"Possibly your recollection may hereafter trouble you. I wish to say that I do not hold you accountable in any way."

That night a wretched creature, half beggar, half worse, was standing on the street under a lamp. A man came along. She glanced at him timidly. He was looking at her, but it would not do to speak to him, he was a gentleman going somewhere. His hands were full of roses. He posted a letter in the box, then to her astonishment he stopped at her side and spoke to her.

"Here are some roses for you," he said, "and here is some money. Go home to-night."

He pushed the roses and money into her hands, and turning, went back up the dim street.

How the Captain Made Christmas

HOW THE CAPTAIN MADE CHRISTMAS

IT was just a few days before Christmas, and the men around the large fireplace at the club had, not unnaturally, fallen to talking of Christmas. They were all men in the prime of life, and all or nearly all of them were from other parts of the country; men who had come to the great city to make their way in life, and who had, on the whole, made it in one degree or another, achieving sufficient success in different fields to allow of all being called successful men. Yet, as the conversation had proceeded, it had taken a reminiscent turn. When it began, only three persons were engaged in it, two of whom, McPheeters and Lesponts, were in lounging-chairs, with their feet stretched out towards the log fire, while the third, Newton, stood with his back to the great hearth, and his coat-tails well divided. The other men were scattered about the room, one or two writing at tables, three or four reading the evening papers, and the rest talking and sipping whiskey and water, or only talking or only sipping whiskey and water. As the conversation proceeded around the fireplace, however, one after another joined the group there, until the circle included every man in the room.

It had begun by Lesponts, who had been looking intently at Newton for some moments as he stood before the fire with his legs well apart and his eyes fastened on the carpet, breaking the silence by asking, suddenly: "Are you going home?"

"I don't know," said Newton, doubtfully, recalled from somewhere in dreamland, but so slowly that a part of his thoughts were still lingering there. "I haven't made up my mind—I'm not sure that I can go so far as Virginia, and I have an invitation to a delightful place—a house-party near here."

"Newton, anybody would know that you were a Virginian," said McPheeters, "by the way you stand before that fire."

Newton said, "Yes," and then, as the half smile the charge had brought up died away, he said, slowly, "I was just thinking how good it felt, and I had gone back and was standing in the old parlor at home the first time I ever noticed my father doing it; I remember getting up and standing by him, a little scrap of a fellow, trying to stand just as he did, and I was feeling the fire, just now, just as I did that night. That was—thirty-three years ago," said Newton, slowly, as if he were doling the years from his memory.

"Newton, is your father living?" asked Lesponts. "No, but my mother is," he said; "she still lives at the old home in the country."

From this the talk had gone on, and nearly all had contributed to it, even the most reticent of them, drawn out by the universal sympathy which the subject had called forth. The great city, with all its manifold interests, was forgotten, and the men of the world went back to their childhood and early life in little villages or on old plantations, and told incidents of the time when the outer world was unknown, and all things had those strange and large proportions which the mind of childhood gives. Old times were ransacked and Christmas experiences in them were given without stint, and the season was voted, without dissent, to have been far ahead of Christmas now. Presently, one of the party said: "Did any of you ever spend a Christmas on the cars? If you have not, thank Heaven, and pray to be preserved from it henceforth, for I've done it, and I tell you it's next to purgatory. I spent one once, stuck in a snow-drift, or almost stuck, for we were ten hours late, and missed all connections, and the Christmas I had expected to spend with friends, I passed in a nasty car with a surly Pullman conductor, an impudent mulatto porter, and a lot of fools, all of whom could have murdered each other, not to speak of a crying baby whose murder was perhaps the only thing all would have united on."

This harsh speech showed that the subject was about exhausted, and someone, a man who had come in only in time to hear the last speaker, had just hazarded the remark, in a faint imitation of an English accent, that the sub-officials in this country were a surly, ill-conditioned lot, anyhow, and always were as rude as they dared to be, when Lesponts, who had looked at the speaker lazily, said:

"Yes, I have spent a Christmas on a sleeping-car, and, strange to say, I have a most delightful recollection of it."

This was surprising enough to have gained him a hearing anyhow, but the memory of the occasion was evidently sufficiently strong to carry Lesponts over obstacles, and he went ahead.

"Has any of you ever taken the night train that goes from here South through the Cumberland and Shenandoah Valleys, or from Washington to strike that train?"

No one seemed to have done so, and he went on:

"Well, do it, and you can even do it Christmas, if you get the right conductor. It's well worth doing the first chance you get, for it's almost the prettiest country in the world that you go through; there is nothing that I've ever seen lovelier than parts of the Cumberland and Shenandoah Valleys, and the New River Valley is just as pretty,—that background of blue beyond those rolling hills, and all,—you know, McPheeters?" McPheeters nodded, and he proceeded:

"I always go that way now when I go South. Well, I went South one winter just at Christmas, and I took that train by accident. I was going to New Orleans to spend Christmas, and had expected to have gotten off to be there several days beforehand, but an unlooked-for matter had turned up and prevented my getting away, and I had given up the idea of going, when I changed my mind: the fact is, I was in a row with a friend of mine there. I decided, on the spur of the moment, to go, anyhow, and thus got off on the afternoon train for Washington, intending to run my luck for getting a sleeper there. This was the day before Christmas-eve and I was due to arrive in New Orleans Christmas-day, some time. Well, when I got to Washington there was not a berth to be had for love or money, and I was in a pickle. I fumed and fussed; abused the railroad companies and got mad with the ticket agent, who seemed, I thought, to be very indifferent as to whether I went to New Orleans or not, and I had just decided to turn around and come back to New York, when the agent, who was making change for someone else, said: 'I'm not positive, but I think there's a train on such and such a road, and you may be able to get a berth on that. It leaves about this time, and if you hurry you may be able to catch it.' He looked at his watch: 'Yes, you've just about time to stand a chance; everything is late to-day, there are such crowds, and the snow and all.' I thanked him, feeling like a dog over my ill-temper and rudeness to him, and decided to try. Anything was better than New York, Christmas-day. So I jumped into a carriage and told the driver to drive like the—the wind, and he did. When we arrived at the station the ticket agent could not tell me whether I could get a berth or not, the conductor had the diagram out at the train, but he thought there was not the slightest chance. I had gotten warmed up, however, by my friend's civility at the other station, and I meant to go if there was any way to do it, so I grabbed up my bags and rushed out of the warm depot into the cold air again. I found the car and the conductor standing outside of it by the steps. The first thing that struck me was his appearance. Instead of being the dapper young naval-officer-ish-looking fellow I was accustomed to, he was a stout, elderly man, with bushy, gray hair and a heavy, grizzled mustache, who looked like an old field-marshal. He was surrounded by quite a number of people all crowding about him and asking him questions at once, some of whose questions he was answering slowly as he pored over his diagram, and others of which he seemed to be ignoring. Some were querulous, some good-natured, and all impatient, but he answered them all with imperturbable good humor. It was very cold, so I pushed my way into the crowd. As I did so I heard him say to someone: ' You asked me if the lower berths were all taken, did you not ? ' ' Yes, five minutes ago ! ' snapped the fellow, whom

I had already heard swearing, on the edge of the circle. 'Well, they are all taken, just as they were the first time I told you they were,' he said, and opened a despatch given him by his porter, a tall, black, elderly negro with gray hair. I pushed my way in and asked him, in my most dulcet tone, if I could get an upper berth to New Orleans. I called him 'Captain,' thinking him a pompous old fellow. He was just beginning to speak to someone else, but I caught him and he looked across the crowd and said 'New Orleans!' My heart sank at the tone, and he went on talking to some other man. 'I told you that I would give you a lower berth, sir, I can give you one now, I have just got a message that the person who had "lower two" will not want it.' 'Hold on, then, I'll take that lower,' called the man who had spoken before, over the crowd, 'I spoke for it first.' 'No you won't,' said the Captain, who went on writing. The man pushed his way in angrily, a big, self-assertive fellow; he was evidently smarting from his first repulse. 'What's that? I did, I say. I was here before that man got here, and asked you for a lower berth, and you said they were all taken.' The Captain stopped and looked at him. 'My dear sir, I know you did; but this gentleman has a lady along.'

But the fellow was angry. 'I don't care,' he said, 'I engaged the berth and I know my rights; I mean to have that lower berth, or I'll see which is bigger, you or Mr. Pullman.' Just then a lady, who had come out on the steps, spoke to the Captain about her seat in the car. He turned to her: 'My dear madam, you are all right, just go in there and take your seat anywhere; when I come in I will fix everything. Go straight into that car and don't come out in this cold air any more.' The lady went back and the old fellow said, 'Nick, go in there and seat that lady, if you have to turn every man out of his seat.' Then, as the porter went in, he turned back to his irate friend. 'Now, my dear sir, you don't mean that: you'd be the first man to give up your berth; this gentleman has his sick wife with him and has been ordered to take her South immediately, and she's going to have a lower berth if I turn every man in that car out, and if you were Mr. Pullman himself I'd tell you the same thing.' The man fell back, baffled and humbled, and we all enjoyed it. Still, I was without a berth, so, with some misgiving, I began: 'Captain?' He turned to me. 'Oh! you want to go to New Orleans?' 'Yes, to spend Christmas; any chance for me?' He looked at his watch. 'My dear young sir,' he said, 'go into the car and take a seat, and I'll do the best I can with you.' I went in, not at all sure that I should get a berth.

"This, of course, was only a part of what went on, but the crowd had gotten into a good humor and was joking, and I had fallen into the same spirit. The first person I looked for when I entered the car was, of course, the sick woman. I soon picked her out: a sweet, frail-looking lady, with that fatal, transparent hue of skin and fine complexion. She was all muffled up, although the car was very warm. Every seat was either occupied or piled high with bags. Well, the train started, and in a little while the Captain came in, and the way that old fellow straightened things out was a revelation. He took charge of the car and ran it as if he had been the Captain of a boat. At first some of the passengers were inclined to grumble, but in a little while they gave in. As for me, I had gotten an upper berth and felt satisfied. When I waked up next morning, however, we were only a hundred and fifty miles from Washington, and were standing still. The next day was Christmas, and every passenger on the train, except the sick lady and her husband, and the Captain, had an engagement for Christmas dinner somewhere a thousand miles away. There had been an accident on the road. The train which was coming north had jumped the track at a trestle and torn a part of it away. Two or three of the trainmen had been hurt. There was no chance of getting by for several hours more. It was a blue party that assembled in the dressing-room, and more than one cursed his luck. One man was talking of suing the company. I was feeling pretty gloomy myself, when the Captain came in. 'Well, gentlemen, 'Christmas-gift'; it's a fine morning, you must go out and taste it,' he said, in a cheery voice, which made me feel fresher and better at once, and which brought a response from every man in the dressing-room. Someone asked promptly how long we should be there. 'I can't tell you, sir, but some little time; several hours. There was a groan. 'You'll have time to go over the battle-field,' said the Captain, still cheerily. 'We are close to the field of one of the bitterest battles of the war.' And then he proceeded to tell us about it briefly. He said, in answer to a question, that he had been in it. 'On which side, Captain?' asked someone. 'Sir!' with some surprise in his voice. 'On which side?' 'On our side, sir, of course.' We decided to go over the field, and after breakfast we did.

"The Captain walked with us over the ground and showed us the lines of attack and defence; pointed out where the heaviest fighting was done, and gave a graphic account of the whole campaign. It was the only battle-field I had ever been over, and I was so much interested that when I got home I read up the campaign, and that set me to reading up on the whole subject of the war. We walked back over the hills, and I never enjoyed a walk more. I felt as if I had got new strength from the cold air. The old fellow stopped at a little house on our way back, and went in whilst we waited. When he came out he had a little bouquet of geranium leaves and lemon verbena which he had got. I had noticed them in the window as we went by, and when I saw the way the sick lady looked when he gave them to her, I wished I had brought them instead of him. Some one intent on knowledge asked him how much he paid for them?

"He said, 'Paid for them! Nothing.'

"'Did you know them before?' he asked.

"'No, sir.' That was all.

"A little while afterwards I saw him asleep in a seat, but when the train started he got up.

"The old Captain by this time owned the car. He was not only an official, he was a host, and he did the honors as if he were in his own house and we were his guests; all was done so quietly and unobtrusively, too; he pulled up a blind here, and drew one down there, just a few inches, 'to give you a little more light on your book, sir';—'to shut out a little of the glare, madam—reading on the cars is a little more trying to the eyes than one is apt to fancy.' He stopped to lean over and tell you that if you looked out of your window you would see what he thought one of the prettiest views in the world; or to mention the fact that on the right was one of the most celebrated old places in the State, a plantation which had once belonged to Colonel So-and-So, 'one of the most remarkable men of his day, sir.'

"His porter, Nicholas, was his admirable second; not a porter at all, but a body-servant; as different from the ordinary Pullman-car porter as light from darkness. In fact, it turned out that he had been an old servant of the Captain's. I happened to speak of him to the Captain, and he said: 'Yes, sir, he's a very good boy; I raised him, or rather, my father did; he comes of a good stock; plenty of sense and know their places. When I came on the road they gave me a mulatto fellow whom I couldn't stand, one of these young, new, "free-issue" some call them, sir, I believe; I couldn't stand him, I got rid of him.' I asked him what was the trouble. 'Oh! no trouble at all, sir; he just didn't know his place, and I taught him. He could read and write a little—a negro is very apt to think, sir, that if he can write he is educated—he could write, and thought he was educated; he chewed a toothpick and thought he was a gentleman. I soon taught him better. He was impertinent, and I put him off the train. After that I told them that I must have my own servant if I was to remain with them, and I got Nick. He is an excellent boy (he was about fifty-five). The black is a capital servant, sir, when he has sense, far better than the mulatto.'

"I became very intimate with the old fellow. You could not help it. He had a way about him that drew you out. I told him I was going to New Orleans to pay a visit to friends there. He said, 'Got a sweetheart there?' I was rather taken aback; but I told him, 'Yes.' He said he knew it as soon as I spoke to him on the platform. He asked me who she was, and I told him her name. He said to me, 'Ah! you lucky dog.' I told him I did not know that I was not most unlucky, for I had no reason to think she was going to marry me. He said, 'You tell her I say you'll be all right.' I felt better, especially when the old chap said, 'I'll tell her so myself.' He knew her. She always travelled with him when she came North, he said.

"I did not know at all that I was all right; in fact, I was rather low down just then about my chances, which was the only reason I was so anxious to go to New Orleans, and I wanted just that encouragement and it helped me mightily. I began to think Christmas on the cars wasn't quite so bad after all. He drew me on, and before I knew it I had told him all about myself. It was the queerest thing; I had no idea in the world of talking about my matters. I had hardly ever spoken of her to a soul; but the old chap had a way of making you feel that he would be certain to understand you, and could help you. He told me about his own case, and it wasn't so different from mine. He lived in Virginia before the war; came from up near Lynchburg somewhere; belonged to an old family there, and had been in love with his sweetheart for years, but could never make any impression on her. She was a beautiful girl, he said, and the greatest belle in the country round. Her father was one of the big lawyers there, and had a fine old place, and the stable was always full of horses of the young fellows who used to be coming to see her, and 'she used to make me sick, I tell you,' he said, 'I used to hate 'em all; I wasn't afraid of 'em; but I used to hate a man to look at her; it seemed so impudent in him; and I'd have been jealous if she had looked at the sun. Well, I didn't know what to do. I'd have been ready to fight 'em all for her, if that would have done any good, but it wouldn't; I didn't have any right to get mad with 'em for loving her, and if I had got into a row she'd have sent me off in a jiffy. But just then the war came on, and it was a Godsend to me. I went in first thing. I made up my mind to go in and fight like five thousand furies, and I thought maybe that would win her, and it did; it worked first-rate. I went in as a private, and I got a bullet through me in about six months, through my right lung, that laid me off for a year or so; then I went back and the boys made me a lieutenant, and when the captain was made a major, I was made captain. I was offered something higher once or twice, but I thought I'd rather stay with my company; I knew the boys, and they knew me, and we had got sort of used to each other—to depending on each other, as it were. The war fixed me all right, though. When I went home that first time my wife had come right around, and as soon as I was well enough we were married. I always said if I could find that Yankee that shot me I'd like to make him a present. I found out that the great trouble with me had been that I had not been bold enough; I used to let her go her own way too much, and seemed to be afraid of her. I *was* afraid of her, too. I bet that's your trouble, sir: are you afraid of her?' I told him I thought I was. ' Well, sir,' he said, ' it will never do; you mustn't let her think that—never. You cannot help being afraid of her, for every man is that; but it is fatal to let her know it. Stand up, sir, stand up for your rights. If you are bound to get down on your knees—and every man feels that he is—don't do it; get up and run out and roll in the dust outside somewhere where she can't see you. Why, sir,' he said, ' it doesn't do to even let her think she's having her own way; half the time she's only testing you, and she doesn't really want what she pretends to want. Of course, I'm speaking of before marriage; after marriage she always wants it, and she's going to have it, anyway, and the sooner you find that out and give in, the better. You must consider this, however, that her way after marriage is always laid down to her with reference to your good. She thinks about you a great deal more than you do about her, and she's always working out something that is for your advantage; she'll let you do some things as you wish, just to make you believe you are having your own way, but she's just been pretending to think otherwise, to make you feel good.'

"This sounded so much like sense that I asked him how much a man ought to stand from a woman. 'Stand, sir?' he said; 'why, everything, everything that does not take away his self-respect.' I said I believed if he'd let a woman do it she'd wipe her shoes on him. 'Why, of course she will,' he said, 'and why shouldn't she? A man is not good enough for a good woman to wipe her shoes on. But if she's the right sort of a woman she won't do it in company, and she won't let others do it at all; she'll keep you for her own wiping.'"

"There's a lot of sense in that, Lesponts," said one of his auditors, at which there was a universal smile of assent. Lesponts said he had found it out, and proceeded.

"Well, we got to a little town in Virginia, I forget the name of it, where we had to stop a short time. The Captain had told me that his home was not far from there, and his old company was raised around there. Quite a number of the old fellows lived about there yet, he said, and he saw some of them nearly every time he passed through, as they 'kept the run of him.' He did not know that he'd 'find any of them out to-day, as it was Christmas, and they would all be at home,' he said. As the train drew up I went out on the platform, however, and there was quite a crowd assembled. I was surprised to find it so quiet, for at other places through which we had passed they had been having high jinks: firing off crackers and making things lively. Here the crowd seemed to be quiet and solemn, and I heard the Captain's name. Just then he came out on the platform, and someone called out: 'There he is, now!' and in a second such a cheer went up as you never heard. They crowded around the old fellow and shook hands with him and hugged him as if he had been a girl."

"I suppose you have reference to the time before you were married," interrupted someone, but Lesponts did not heed him. He went on:

"It seemed the rumor had got out that morning that it was the Captain's train that had gone off the track and that the Captain had been killed in the wreck, and this crowd had assembled to meet the body. 'We were going to give you a big funeral, Captain,' said one old fellow; 'they've got you while you are living, but we claim you when you are dead. We ain't going to let 'em have you then. We're going to put you to sleep in old Virginia.'

"The old fellow was much affected, and made them a little speech. He introduced us to them all. He said: 'Gentlemen, these are my boys, my neighbors and family;' and then, 'Boys, these are my friends; I don't know all their names yet, but they are my friends.' And we were. He rushed off to send a telegram to his wife in New Orleans, because, as he said afterwards, she, too, might get hold of the report that he had been killed; and a Christmas message would set her up, anyhow. She'd be a little low down at his not getting there, he said, as he had never missed a Christmas-day at home since '64.

"When dinner-time came he was invited in by pretty nearly everyone in the car, but he declined; he said he had to attend to a matter. I was going in with a party, but I thought the old fellow would be lonely, so I waited and insisted on his dining with me. I found that it had occurred to him that a bowl of eggnogg would make it seem more like Christmas, and he had telegraphed ahead to a friend at a little place to have 'the materials' ready. Well, they were on hand when we got there, and we took them aboard, and the old fellow made one of the finest eggnoggs you ever tasted in your life. The rest of the passengers had no idea of what was going on, and when the old chap came in with a big bowl, wreathed in holly, borne by Nick, and the old Captain marching behind, there was quite a cheer. It was offered to the ladies first, of course, and then the men assembled in the smoker and the Captain did the honors. He did them handsomely, too : made us one of the prettiest little speeches you ever heard ; said that Christmas was not dependent on the fireplace, however much a roaring fire might contribute to it ; that it was in everyone's heart and might be enjoyed as well in a railway-car as in a hall, and that in this time of change and movement it behooved us all to try and keep up what was good and cheerful and bound us together, and to remember that Christmas was not only a time for merry-making, but was the time when the Saviour of the world came among men to bring peace and good-will, and that we should remember all our friends everywhere. 'And, gentlemen,' he said, ' there are two toasts I always like to propose at this time, and which I will ask you to drink. The first is to my wife.' It was drunk, you may believe. And the second is, 'My friends: all mankind.' This too, was drunk, and just then someone noticed that the old fellow had nothing but a little water in his glass. 'Why, Captain,' he said, 'you are not drinking! that is not fair.' 'Well, no, sir,' said the old fellow, 'I never drink anything on duty; you see it is one of the regulations and I subscribed them, and, of course, I could not break my word. Nick, there, will drink my share, however, when you are through; he isn't held up to quite such high accountability.' And sure enough, Nick drained off a glass and made a speech which got him a handful of quarters. Well, of course, the old Captain owned not only the car, but all in it by this time, and we spent one of the jolliest evenings you ever saw. The glum fellow who had insisted on his rights at Washington made a little speech, and paid the Captain one of the prettiest compliments I ever heard. He said he had discovered that the Captain had given him his own lower berth after he had been so rude to him, and that instead of taking his upper berth as he had supposed he would have done, he had given that to another person and had sat up himself all night. That was I. The old fellow had given the grumbler his 'lower' in the smoking-room, and had given me his 'upper.' The fellow made him a very handsome apology before us all, and the Captain had his own berth that night, you may believe.

"Well, we were all on the *qui vive* to see the Captain's wife when we got to New Orleans. The Captain had told us that she always came down to the station to meet him; so we were all on the lookout for her. He told me the first thing that he did was to kiss her, and then he went and filed his reports, and then they went home together, 'And if you'll come and dine with me,' he said to me, 'I'll give you the best dinner you ever had — real old Virginia cooking; Nick's wife is our only servant, and she is an excellent cook.' I promised him to go one day, though I could not go the first day. Well, the meeting between the old fellow and his wife was worth the trip to New Orleans to see. I had formed a picture in my mind of a queenly looking woman, a Southern matron— you know how you do? And when we drew into the station I looked around for her. As I did not see her, I watched the Captain. He got off, and I missed him in the crowd. Presently, though, I saw him and I asked him, 'Captain, is she here?' 'Yes, sir, she is, she never misses; that's the sort of a wife to have, sir; come here and let me introduce you.''

He pulled me up and introduced me to a sweet little old lady, in an old, threadbare dress and wrap, and a little, faded bonnet, whom I had seen as we came up, watching eagerly for someone, but whom I had not thought of as being possibly the Captain's grand-dame. The Captain's manner, however, was beautiful. 'My dear, this is my friend, Mr. Lesponts, and he has promised to come and dine with us,' he said, with the air of a lord, and then he leaned over and whispered something to her. 'Why, she's coming to dine with us to-day,' she said with a very cheery laugh; and then she turned and gave me a look that swept me from top to toe, as if she were weighing me to see if I'd do. I seemed to pass, for she came forward and greeted me with a charming cordiality, and invited me to dine with them, saying that her husband had told her I knew Miss So-and-So, and she was coming that day, and if I had no other engagement they would be very glad if I would come that day, too. Then she turned to the Captain and said, 'I saved Christmas dinner for you; for when you didn't come I knew the calendar and all the rest of the world were wrong; so to-day is our Christmas.'

—"Well, that's all," said Lesponts; "I did not mean to talk so much, but the old Captain

How the Captain Made Christmas

is such a character, I wish you could know him. You'd better believe I went, and I never had a nicer time. They were just as poor as they could be, in one way, but in another they were rich. He had a sweet little home in their three rooms. I found that my friend always dined with them one day in the Christmas-week, and I happened to hit that day." He leaned back.

"That was the beginning of my good fortune," he said, slowly, and then stopped. Most of the party knew Lespont's charming wife, so no further explanation was needed. One of them said presently, however, "Lesponts, why didn't you fellows get him some better place?"

"He was offered a place," said Lesponts. "The fellow who had made the row about the lower berth turned out to be a great friend of the head of the Pullman Company, and he got him the offer of a place at three times the salary he got, but after consideration, he declined it. He would have had to come North, and he said that he could not do that: his wife's health was not very robust and he did not know how she could stand the cold climate; then, she had made her friends, and she was too old to try to make a new set; and finally, their little girl was buried there, and they did not want to leave her; so he declined. When she died, he said, or whichever one of them died first, the other would come back home to the old place in Virginia, and bring the other two with him, so they could all be at home together again. Meantime, they were very comfortable and well satisfied."

There was a pause after Lesponts ended, and then one of the fellows rang the bell and said, "Let's drink the old Captain's health," which was unanimously agreed to. Newton walked over to a table and wrote a note, and then slipped out of the club; and when next day I inquired after him of the boy at the door, he said he had left word to tell anyone who asked for him, that he would not be back till after Christmas; that he had gone home to Virginia. Several of the other fellows went off home too, myself among them, and I was glad I did, for I heard one of the men say he never knew the club so deserted as it was that Christmas-day.

Little Darby

LITTLE DARBY

I

THE County had been settled as a "frontier" in early colonial days, and when it ceased to be frontier, settlement had taken a jump beyond it, and in a certain sense over it, to the richer lands of the Piedmont. When, later on, steam came, the railway simply cut across it at its narrowest part, and then skirted along just inside its border on the bank of the little river which bounded it on the north, as if it intentionally left it to one side. Thus, modern progress had not greatly interfered with it either for good or bad, and its development was entirely natural.

It was divided into "neighborhoods," a name in itself implying something both of its age and origin; for the population was old, and the customs of life and speech were old likewise.

This chronicle, however, is not of the "neighborhoods," for they were known, or may be known by any who will take the trouble to plunge boldly in and throw themselves on the hospitality of any of the dwellers therein. It is rather of the unknown tract, which lay vague and undefined in between the several neighborhoods of the upper end. The history of the former is known both in peace and in war: in the pleasant homesteads which lie on the hills above the little rivers which make down through the county to join the great river below, and in the long list of those who fell in battle, and whose names are recorded on the slabs set up by their comrades on the walls of the old Court House. The history of the latter, however, is unrecorded. The lands were in the main very poor and grown up in pine, or else, where the head-waters of a little stream made down in a number of "branches," were swampy and malarial. Possibly it was this poverty of the soil or unwholesomeness of their location, which more than anything else kept the people of this district somewhat distinct from others around them, however poor they might be. They dwelt in their little cabins among their pines, or down on the edges of the swampy district, distinct both from the gentlemen on their old plantations and from the sturdy farmer-folk who owned the smaller places. What title they had to their lands originally, or how they traced it back, or where they had come from, no one knew. They had been there from time immemorial, as long or longer, if anything, than the owners of the plantations about them; and insignificant as they were, they were not the kind to attempt to question, even had anyone been inclined to do so, which no one was.

They had the names of the old English gentry, and were a clean-limbed, blond, blue-eyed people.

When they were growing to middle age, their life told on them and made them weather-beaten, and not infrequently hard-visaged; but when they were young there were often among them straight, supple young fellows with clear-cut features, and lithe, willowy-looking girls, with pink faces and blue, or brown, or hazel eyes, and a mien which one might have expected to find in a hall rather than in a cabin.

Darby Stanley and Cove Mills (short for Coverley) were the leaders of the rival factions of the district. They lived as their fathers had lived before them, on opposite sides of the little stream, the branches of which crept through the alder and gum thickets between them, and contributed to make the district almost as impenetrable to the uninitiated as a mountain fastness. The long log-cabin of the Cove-Millses, where room had been added to room in a straight line, until it looked like the side of a log fort, peeped from its pines across at the clearing where the hardly more pretentious home of Darby Stanley was set back amid a little orchard of ragged peach-trees, and half hidden under a great wistaria vine. But though the two places lay within rifle shot of each other, they were almost as completely divided as if the big river below had rolled between them. Since the great fight between old Darby and Cove Mills over Henry Clay, there had rarely been an election in which some members of the two families had not had a "clinch." They had to be thrown together sometimes "at meeting," and their children now and then met down on the river fishing, or at "the washing hole," as the deep place in the little stream below where the branches ran together, was called; but they held themselves as much aloof from each other as their higher neighbors, the Hampdens and the Douwills, did on their plantations. The children, of course, would "run together," nor did the parents take steps to prevent them, sure that they would, as they grew up, take their own sides as naturally as they themselves had done in their day. Meantime "children were children," and they need not be worried with things like grown-up folk.

When Aaron Hall died and left his little farm and all his small belongings to educate free the children of his poor neighbors, the farmers about availed themselves of his benefaction, and the children for six miles around used to attend the little school which was started in the large hewn-log school-house on the roadside known as "Hall's Free School." Few people knew the plain, homely, hard-working man, or wholly understood him. Some thought him stingy, some weak-minded, some only queer, and at first his benefaction was hardly comprehended; but in time quite a little oasis began about the little fountain, which the poor farmer's bequest had opened under the big oaks by the wayside, and gradually its borders extended, until finally it penetrated as far as the district, and Cove Mills's children appeared one morning at the door of the little school-house, and, with sheepish faces and timid voices, informed the teacher that their father had sent them to school.

At first there was some debate over at Darby Stanley's place, whether they should show their contempt for the new departure of the Millses, by standing out against them, or should follow their example. It was hard for a Stanley to have to follow a Mills in anything. So they stood out for a year. As it seemed, however, that the Millses were getting something to which the Stanleys were as much entitled as they, one morning little Darby Stanley walked in at the door, and without taking his hat off, announced that he had come to go to school. He was about fifteen at the time, but he must have been nearly six feet (his sobriquet being wholly due to the fact that Big Darby was older, not taller), and though he was spare, there was something about his face as he stood in the open door, or his eye as it rested defiantly on the teacher's face, which prevented more than a general buzz of surprise.

"Take off your hat," said the teacher, and he took it off slowly. "I suppose you can read?" was the first question.

"No."

A snicker ran round the room, and little Darby's brow clouded.

As he not only could not read, but could not even spell, and in fact did not know his letters, he was put into the alphabet class, the class of the smallest children in the school.

Little Darby walked over to the corner indicated with his head up, his hands in his pockets, and a roll in his gait full of defiance, and took his seat on the end of the bench and looked straight before him. He could hear the titter around him, and a lowering look came into his blue eyes. He glanced sideways down the bench opposite. It happened that the next seat to his was that of Vashti Mills, who was at that time just nine. She was not laughing, but was looking at Darby earnestly, and as he caught her eye she nodded to him, "Good-mornin'." It was the first greeting the boy had received, and though he returned it sullenly, it warmed him, and the cloud passed from his brow and presently he looked at her again. She handed him a book. He took it and looked at it as if it were something that might explode.

He was not an apt scholar; perhaps he had begun too late; perhaps there was some other cause; but though he could swim better, climb better, and run faster than any boy in the school, or, for that matter, in the county, and knew the habits of every bird that flitted through the woods and of every animal that lived in the district, he was not good at his books. His mind was on other things. When he had spent a week over the alphabet, he did know a letter as such, but only by the places on the page they were on, and gave up when "big A" was shown him on another page, only asking how in the dickens "big A" got over there. He pulled off his coat silently whenever ordered and took his whippings like a lamb, without a murmur and almost without flinching, but every boy in the school learned that it was dangerous to laugh at him; and though he could not learn to read fluently or to train his fingers to guide a pen, he could climb the tallest pine in the district to get a young crow for Vashti, and could fashion all sorts of curious whistles, snares, and other contrivances with his long fingers.

He did not court popularity, was rather cold and unapproachable, and Vashti Mills was about the only other scholar with whom he seemed to be on warm terms. Many a time when the tall boy stood up before the thin teacher, helpless and dumb over some question which almost anyone in the school could answer, the little girl, twisting her fingers in an ecstacy of anxiety, whispered to him the answer in the face of almost certain detection and of absolutely certain punishment. In return, he worshipped the ground she walked on, and whichever side Vashti was on, Darby was sure to be on it too. He climbed the tallest trees to get her nuts; waded into the miriest swamps to find her more brilliant nosegays of flowers than the other girls had; spent hours to gather rarer birds' eggs than they had, and was everywhere and always her silent worshipper and faithful champion. They soon learned that the way to secure his help in anything was to get Vashti Mills to ask it, and the little girl quickly discovered her power and used it as remorselessly over her tall slave as any other despot ever did. They were to be seen any day trailing along the plantation paths which the school-children took from the district, the others in a clump, and the tall boy and little calico-clad girl, who seemed in summer mainly sun-bonnet and bare legs, either following or going before the others at some distance.

The death of Darby—of old Darby, as he had begun to be called—cut off Little Darby from his "schoolin'," in the middle of his third year, and before he had learned more than to read and cipher a little and to write in a scrawly fashion; for he had been rather irregular in his attendance at all times. He now stopped altogether, giving the teacher as his reason, with characteristic brevity: "Got to work."

Perhaps no one at the school mourned the long-legged boy's departure except his little friend Vashti, now a well-grown girl of twelve, very straight and slim and with big dark eyes. She gave him when he went away the little Testament she had gotten as a prize, and which was one of her most cherished possessions. Other boys found the first honor as climber, runner, rock-flinger, wrestler, swimmer, and fighter open once more to them, and were free from the silent and somewhat contemptuous gaze of him who, however they looked down on him, was a sort of silent power among them. Vashti alone felt a void and found by its sudden absence how great a force was the steady backing of one who could always be counted on to take one's side without question. She had to bear the gibes of the school as "Miss Darby," and though her two brothers were ready enough to fight for her if boys pushed her too hardly, they could do nothing against girls, and the girls were her worst tormentors.

The name was fastened on her, and it clung to her until, as time went on, she came to almost hate the poor innocent cause of it.

Meantime Darby, beginning to fill out and take on the shoulders and form of a man, began to fill also the place of the man in his little home. This among other things meant opposition, if not hostility, to everything on Cove Mills's side. When old Darby died the Millses all went to the funeral, of course; but that did not prevent their having the same feeling toward Little Darby afterward, and the breach continued.

At first he used to go over occasionally to see Vashti and carry her little presents, as he had done at school; but he soon found that it was not the same thing. He was always received coolly, and shortly he was given to understand that he was not wanted there, and in time Vashti herself showed that she was not the same she had been to him before. Thus the young fellow was thrown back on himself, and the hostility between the two cabins was as great as ever.

He spent much of his time in the woods, for the Stanley place was small at best, only a score or so of acres, and mostly covered with pines, and Little Darby was but a poor hand at working with a hoe — their only farm implement. He was, however, an unerring shot, with an eye like a hawk to find a squirrel flat on top of the grayest limb of the tallest hickory in the woods, or a hare in her bed among the brownest broomsedge in the county, and he knew the habits of fish and bird and animal as if he had created them; and though he could not or would not handle a hoe, he was the best hand at an axe "in the stump," in the district, and Mrs. Stanley was kept in game if not in meal.

The Millses dilated on his worthlessness, and Vashti, grown to be a slender slip of a girl with very bright eyes and a little nose, was loudest against him in public; though rumor said she had fallen afoul of her youngest brother and boxed his jaws for seconding something she had said of him.

The Mills's enmity was well understood, and there were not wanting those to take Darby's side. He had grown to be the likeliest young man in the district, tall, and straight as a sapling, and though Vashti flaunted her hate of him and turned up her little nose more than it was already turned up at his name, there were many other girls in the pines who looked at him languishingly from under their long sunbonnets, and thought he was worth both the Mills boys and Vashti to boot. So when at a fish-fry the two Mills boys attacked him and he whipped them both together, some said it served them right, while others declared they did just what they ought to have done, and intimated that Darby was less anxious to meet their father than he was them, who were nothing more than boys to him. These asked in proof of their view, why he had declined to fight when Old Cove had abused him so to his face. This was met by the fact that he "could not have been so mighty afeared," for he had jumped in and saved Chris. Mills's life ten minutes afterward, when he got beyond his depth in the pond and had already sunk twice. But, then, to be sure, it had to be admitted that he was the best swimmer on the ground, and that any man there would have gone in to save his worst enemy if he had been drowning. This must have been the view that Vashti Mills took of the case; for one day not long afterward, having met Darby at the cross-roads store where she was looking at some pink calico, and where he had come to get some duck-shot and waterproof caps, she turned on him publicly, and with flashing eyes and mantling cheeks, gave him to understand that if she were a man he "would not have had to fight two boys," and he would not have come off so well either. If anything, this attack brought Darby friends, for he not only had whipped the Mills boys fairly, and had fought only when they had pressed him, but had, as has been said, declined to fight old man Mills under gross provocation; and besides, though they were younger than he, the Mills boys were seventeen and eighteen, and "not such babies either; if they insisted on fighting they had to take what they got and not send their sister to talk and abuse a man about it afterward." And the weight of opinion was that, "that Vashti Mills was gettin' too airified and set up anyways."

All this reached Mrs. Stanley, and was no doubt sweet to her ears. She related it in her drawling voice to Darby as he sat in the door one evening, but it did not seem to have much effect on him; he never stirred or showed by word or sign that he even heard her, and finally, without speaking, he rose and lounged away into the woods. The old woman gazed after him silently until he disappeared, and then gave a look across to where the Mills cabin peeped from among the pines, which was full of hate.

. . . . . .

The fish-fry at which Darby Stanley had first fought the Mills boys and then pulled one of them out of the river, had been given by one of the county candidates for election as delegate to a convention which was to be held at the capital, and possibly the division of sentiment in the district between the Millses and Little Darby was as much due to political as to personal feeling; for the sides were growing more and more tightly drawn, and the

Millses, as usual, were on one side and Little Darby on the other; and both sides had strong adherents. The question was on one side, Secession, with probable war; and on the other, the Union as it was. The Millses were for the candidate who advocated the latter, and Little Darby was for him who wanted secession. Both candidates were men of position and popularity, the one a young man and the other older, and both were neighbors.

The older man was elected, and shortly the question became imminent, and all the talk about the Cross-roads was of war. As time had worn on, Little Darby, always silent, had become more and more so, and seemed to be growing morose. He spent more and more of his time in the woods or about the Cross-roads, the only store and post-office near the district where the little tides of the quiet life around used to meet. At length Mrs. Stanley considered it so serious that she took it upon herself to go over and talk to her neighbor, Mrs. Douwill, as she generally did on matters too intricate and grave for the experience of the district. She found Mrs. Douwill, as always, sympathetic and kind, and though she took back with her not much enlightenment as to the cause of her son's trouble or its cure, she went home in a measure comforted with the assurance of the sympathy of one stronger than she. She had found out that her neighbor, powerful and rich as she seemed to her to be, had her own troubles and sorrows; she heard from her of the danger of war breaking out at any time, and her husband would enlist among the first.

Little Darby did not say much when his mother told of her visit; but his usually downcast eyes had a new light in them, and he began to visit the Cross-roads oftener.

At last one day the news that came to the Cross-roads was that there was to be war. It had been in the air for some time, but now it was undoubted. It came in the presence of Mr. Douwill himself, who had come the night before and was commissioned by the Governor to raise a company. There were a number of people there—quite a crowd for the little Cross-roads—for the stir had been growing day by day, and excitement and anxiety were on the increase. The papers had been full of secession, firing on flags, raising troops, and everything; but that was far off. When Mr. Douwill appeared in person it came nearer, though still few, if any, quite took it in that it could be actual and immediate. Among those at the Cross-roads that day were the Millses, father and sons, who looked a little critically at the speaker as one who had always been on the other side. Little Darby was also there, silent as usual, but with a light burning in his blue eyes.

That evening, when Little Darby reached home, which he did somewhat earlier than usual, he announced to his mother that he had enlisted as a soldier. The old woman was standing before her big fireplace when he told her, and she leaned against it quite still for a moment; then she sat down, stumbling a little on the rough hearth as she made her way to her little broken chair. Darby got up and found her a better one, which she took without a word.

Whatever entered into her soul in the little cabin that night, when Mrs. Stanley went among her neighbors she was a soldier's mother. She even went over to Cove Mills's on some pretext connected with Darby's going. Vashti was not at home, but Mrs. Mills was, and she felt a sudden loss, as if somehow the Millses had fallen below the Stanleys. She talked of it for several days; she could not make out entirely what it was. Vashti's black eyes flashed.

The next day Darby went to the Cross-roads to drill; there was, besides the recruits, who were of every class, quite a little crowd there to look at the drill. Among them were two women of the poorest class, one old and faded, rather than gray, the other hardly better dressed, though a slim figure, straight and trim, gave her a certain distinction, even had not a few ribbons and a little ornament or two on her pink calico, with a certain air, showed that she was accustomed to being admired.

The two women found themselves together once during the day, and their eyes met. It was just as the line of soldiers passed. Those of the elder lighted with a sudden spark of mingled triumph and hate, those of the younger flashed back for a moment and then fell beneath the elder's gaze. There was much enthusiasm about the war, and among others, both of the Mills boys enlisted before the day was ended, their sister going in with them to the room where their names were entered on the roll, and coming out with flashing eyes and mantling cheeks. She left the place earlier than most of the crowd, but not until after the drill was over and some of the young soldiers had gone home. The Mills boys' enlistment was set down in the district to Vashti, and some said it was because she was jealous of Little Darby being at the end of the company, with a new gun and such a fine uniform; for her hatred of Little Darby was well known; anyhow, their example was followed, and in a short time nearly all the young men in the district had enlisted.

At last one night a summons came for the company to assemble at the Cross-roads next day with arms and equipment. Orders had come for them to report at once at the capital of the State for drill, before being sent into the field to repel a force which, report said, was already on the way to invade the State. There was the greatest excitement and enthusiasm. This was war! And everyone was ready to meet it. The day was given to taking an inventory of arms and equipment, and then there was a drill, and then the company was dismissed for the night, as many of them had families of whom they had not taken leave, and as they had not come that day prepared to leave, and were ordered to join the commander next day, prepared to march.

Little Darby escorted his mother home, taciturn as ever. At first there was quite a company; but as they went their several ways to their home, at last Little Darby and his mother were left alone in the piney path, and made the last part of their way alone. Now and then the old woman's eyes were on him, and often his eyes were on her, but they did not speak; they just walked on in silence till they reached home.

It was but a poor, little house even when the wistaria vine covered it, wall and roof, and the bees hummed among its clusters of violet blossoms; but now the wistaria bush was only a tangle of twisted wires hung upon it, and the little weather-stained cabin looked bare and poor enough. As the young fellow stood in the door looking out with the evening light upon him, his tall, straight figure filled it as if it had been a frame. He stood perfectly motionless for some minutes, gazing across the gum thickets before him.

The sun had set only about a half-hour and the light was still lingering on the under edges of the clouds in the west and made a sort of glow in the little yard before him, as it did in front of the cabin on the other hill. His eye first swept the well-known horizon, taking in the thickets below him and the heavy pines on either side where it was already dusk, and then rested on the little cabin opposite. Whether he saw it or not, one could hardly have told, for his face wore a reminiscent look. Figures moved backward and forward over there, came out and went in, without his look changing. Even Vashti, faintly distinguishable in her gay dress, came out and passed down the hill alone, without his expression changing. It was, perhaps, fifteen minutes later that he seemed to awake, and after a look over his shoulder stepped from the door into the yard. His mother was cooking, and he strolled down the path across the little clearing and entered the pines. Insensibly his pace quickened—he strode along the dusky path with as firm a step as if it were broad daylight. A quarter of a mile below the path crossed the little stream and joined the path from Cove Mills's place, which he used to take when he went to school. He crossed at the old log and turned down the path through the little clearing there. The next moment he stood face to face with Vashti Mills. Whether he was surprised or not no one could have told, for he said not a word, and his face was in the shadow, though Vashti's was toward the clearing and the light from the sky was on it. Her hat was in her hand. He stood still, but did not stand aside to let her pass, until she made an imperious little gesture and stepped as if she would have passed around him. Then he stood aside. But she did not appear in a hurry to avail herself of the freedom offered, she simply looked at him. He took off his cap sheepishly enough, and said, "Good-evenin'."

"Good-evenin'," she said, and then, as the pause became embarrassing, she said, "Hear you're agoin' away to-morrer?"

"Yes—to-morrer mornin'."

"When you're acomin' back?" she asked, after a pause in which she had been twisting the pink string of her hat.

"Don't know—may be never." Had he been looking at her he might have seen the change which his words brought to her face; she lifted her eyes to his face for the first time since the half defiant glance she had given him when they met, and they had a strange light in them, but at the moment he was looking at a bow on her dress which had been pulled loose. He put out his hand and touched it and said:

"You're a-losin' yer bow," and as she found a pin and fastened it again, he added, "An' I don' know as anybody keers."

An overpowering impulse changed her and forced her to say: "I don't know as anybody does either; I know as I don't."

The look on his face smote her, and the spark died out of her eyes as he said, slowly: "No, I knowed you didn'! I don't know as anybody does, exceptin' my old woman. Maybe she will a little. I jist wanted to tell you that I wouldn't a' fit them boys if they hadn't a' pushed me so hard, and I wan't afeared to fight your old man, I jist wouldn't — that's all."

What answer she might have made to this was prevented by him; for he suddenly held out his hand with something in it, saying, "Here."

She instinctively reached out to take whatever it was, and he placed in her hand a book which she recognized as the little Testament which she had won as a prize at school and had given him when they went to school together. It was the only book she had ever possessed as her very own.

"I brought this thinking as how maybe you might 'a'-wanted—me to keep it," he was going to say; but he checked himself and said: "might 'a'-wanted it back."

Before she could recover from the surprise of finding the book in her hand her own, he was gone. The words only came to her clearly as his retreating footsteps grew fainter and his tall figure faded in the darkening light. She made a hasty step or two after him, then checked herself and listened intently to see if he were not returning, and then, as only the katydids answered, threw herself flat on the ground and grovelled in the darkness.

There were few houses in the district or in the county where lights did not burn all that night. The gleam of the fire in Mrs. Stanley's little house could be seen all night from the door of the Mills cabin, as the candle by which Mrs. Mills complained while she and Vashti sewed, could be faintly seen from Little Darby's house. The two Mills boys slept stretched out on the one bed in the little centre-room.

While the women sewed and talked fitfully by the single tallow candle, and old Cove dozed in a chair with his long legs stretched out toward the fire and the two shining barrels of his sons' muskets resting against his knees, where they had slipped from his hands when he had finished rubbing them.

The younger woman did most of the sewing. Her fingers were suppler than her mother's, and she scarcely spoke except to answer the latter's querulous questions. Presently a rooster crowed somewhere in the distance, and almost immediately another crowed in answer closer at hand.

"Thar's the second rooster-crow, it's gittin' erlong toward the mornin'," said the elder woman.

The young girl made no answer, but a moment later rose and, laying aside the thing she was sewing, walked to the low door and stepped out into the night. When she returned and picked up her sewing again, her mother said:

"I de-clar, Vashti, you drinks mo' water than anybody I ever see."

To which she made no answer.

"Air they a-stirrin' over at Mis's Stanley's?" asked the mother.

"They ain't a-been to bed," said the girl, quietly; and then, as if a sudden thought had struck her, she hitched her chair nearer the door which she had left open, and sat facing it as she sewed on the brown thing she was working on a small bow which she took from her dress.

"I de-clar, I don't see what old Mis's Stanley is actually a-gwine to do," broke out Mrs. Mills, suddenly, and when Vashti did not feel called on to try to enlighten her she added, "Do you?"

"Same as other folks, I s'pose," said the girl, quietly.

"Other folks has somebody—somebody to take keer on 'em. I've got your pappy now; but she ain't got nobody but little Darby—and when he's gone what will she do?"

For answer Vashti only hitched her chair a

little nearer the door and sewed on almost in darkness. "Not that he was much account to her, ner to anybody else, except for goin' aroun' a-fightin' and a-fussin'."

"He was account to her," flamed up the girl, suddenly; "he was account to her, to her and to everybody else. He was the fust soldier that 'listed, and he's account to everybody."

The old woman had raised her head in astonishment at her daughter's first outbreak, and was evidently about to reply sharply; but the girl's flushed face and flashing eyes awed and silenced her.

"Well, well, I ain't sayin' nothin' against him," she said, presently.

"Yes, you air—you're always sayin' somethin' against him—and so is everybody else—and they ain't fitten to tie his shoes. Why don't they say it to his face! There ain't one of 'em as dares it, and he's the best soldier in the comp'ny, an' I'm jest as proud of it as if he was my own."

The old woman was evidently bound to defend herself. She said:

"It don't lay in your mouth to take up for him, Vashti Mills; for you're the one as has gone up and down and abused him scandalous."

"Yes, and I know I did," said the girl, springing up excitedly and tossing her arms and tearing at her ribbons. "An' I told him to his face too, and that's the only good thing about it. I knowed it was a lie when I told him, and he knowed it was a lie too, and he knowed I knowed it was a lie—what's more—and I'm glad he did—fo' God I'm glad he did. He could 'a' whipped the whole company an' he jest wouldn't—an' that's God's truth—God's fatal truth."

The next instant she was on her knees hunting for something on the floor, in an agony of tears; and as her father, aroused by the noise, rose and asked a question, she sprang up and rushed out of the door.

The sound of an axe was already coming through the darkness across the gum thickets from Mrs. Stanley's, telling that preparation was being made for Darby's last breakfast. It might have told more, however, by its long continuance; for it meant that Little Darby was cutting his mother a supply of wood to last till his return. Inside, the old woman, thin and faded, was rubbing his musket.

. . . .

The sun was just rising above the pines, filling the little bottom between the cabins with a

Little Darby

sort of rosy light, and making the dewy bushes and weeds sparkle with jewel-strung gossamer webs, when Little Darby, with his musket in his hand, stepped for the last time out of the low door. He had been the first soldier in the district to enlist, he must be on time. He paused just long enough to give one swift glance around the little clearing, and then set out along the path at his old swinging pace. At the edge of the pines he turned and glanced back. His mother was standing in the door, but whether she saw him or not he could not tell. He waved his hand to her, but she did not wave back, her eyes were failing somewhat. The next instant he disappeared in the pines.

He had crossed the little stream on the old log and passed the point where he had met Vashti the evening before, when he thought he heard something fall a little ahead of him. It could not have been a squirrel, for it did not move after it fell. His old hunter's instinct caused him to look keenly down the path as he turned the clump of bushes which stopped his view; but he saw no squirrel or other moving thing. The only thing he saw was a little brown something with a curious spot on it lying in the path some little way ahead. As he came nearer it, he saw that it was a small parcel not as big as a man's fist. Someone had evidently dropped it the evening before. He picked it up and examined it as he strode along. It was a little case or wallet made of some brown stuff, such as women carry needles and thread in, and it was tied up with a bit of red, white and blue string, the Confederate colors, on the end of which was sewed a small bow of pink ribbon. He untied it. It was what it looked to be: a roughly made little needle-case such as women use, tolerably well stocked with sewing materials, and it had something hard and almost square in a separate pocket. Darby opened this, and his gun almost slipped from his hand. Inside was the Testament he had given back to Vashti the evening before. He stopped stock-still, and gazed at it in amazement, turning it over in his hand. He recognized the bow of pink ribbon as one like that which she had had on her dress the evening before. She must have dropped it. Then it came to him that she must have given it to one of her brothers, and a pang shot through his heart. But how did it get where he found it? He was too keen a woodsman not to know that no footstep had gone before his on that path that morning. It was a mystery too deep for him, and after puzzling over it a while he tied the parcel up again as nearly like what it had been before as he could, and determined to give it to one of the Mills boys when he reached the Cross-roads. He unbuttoned his jacket and put it into the little inner pocket, and then rebuttoning it carefully, stepped out again more briskly than before.

It was perhaps an hour later that the Mills boys set out for the Cross-roads. Their father and mother went with them; but Vashti did not go. She had "been out to look for the cow," and got in only just before they left, still clad in her yesterday's finery; but it was wet and bedraggled with the soaking dew. When they were gone she sat down in the door, limp and dejected.

More than once during the morning the girl rose and started down the path as if she would follow them and see the company set out on its march, but each time she came back and sat down again in the door, remaining there for a good while as if in thought.

Once she went over almost to Mrs. Stanley's, then turned back and sat down again.

So the morning passed, and the first thing she knew, her father and mother had returned. The company had started. They were to march to the bridge that night. She heard them talking over the appearance that they had made; the speech of the captain; the cheers that went up as they marched off—the enthusiasm of the crowd. Her father was in much excitement. Suddenly she seized her sun-bonnet and slipped out of the house and across the clearing, and the next instant she was flying down the path through the pines. She knew the road they had taken, and a path that would strike it several miles lower down. She ran like a deer, up hill and down, availing herself of every short cut, until, about an hour after she started, she came out on the road. Fortunately for her, the delays incident to getting any body of new troops on the march had detained the company, and a moment's inspection of the road showed her that they had not yet passed. Clambering up a bank, she concealed herself and lay down. In a few moments she heard the noise they made in the distance, and she was still panting from her haste when they came along, the soldiers marching in order, as if still on parade, and a considerable company of friends attending them. Not a man, however, dreamed that, flat on her face in the bushes, lay a girl peering down at them with her breath held, but with a heart which beat so loud to her own ears that she felt they must hear it. Least of all did Darby Stanley, marching erect and tall in front, for all the sore heart in his bosom, know that her eyes were on him as long as she could see him.

When Vashti brought up the cow that night it was later than usual. It perhaps was fortunate for her that the change made by the absence of the boys prevented any questioning. After all the excitement her mother was in a fit of despondency. Her father sat in the door looking straight before him, as silent as the pine on which his vacant gaze was fixed. Even when the little cooking they had was through with and his supper was offered him, he never spoke. He ate in silence and then took his seat again. Even Mrs. Mills's complaining about the cow straying so far brought no word from him any more than from Vashti. He sat silent as before, his long legs stretched out toward the fire. The glow of the embers fell on the rough, thin face and lit it up, bringing out the features and making them suddenly clear-cut and strong. It might have been only the fire, but there seemed the glow of something more, and the eyes burnt back under the shaggy brows. The two women likewise were silent, the elder now and then casting a glance at her husband. She offered him his pipe, but he said nothing, and silence fell as before.

Presently she could stand it no longer. "I de-clar, Vashti," she said, "I believe your pappy takes it most harder than I does."

The girl made some answer about the boys. It was hardly intended for him to hear, but he rose suddenly, and walking to the door, took down from the two dogwood forks above it his old, long, single-barrelled gun, and turning to his wife said, "Git me my coat, old woman; by Gawd, I'm a-gwine." The two women were both on their feet in a second. Their faces were white and their hands were clenched under the sudden stress, their breath came fast. The older woman was the first to speak.

"What in the worl' ken you do, Cove Mills, ole an' puny as you is, an' got the rheumatiz all the time, too?"

"I ken pint a gun," said the old man, doggedly, "an' I'm a-gwine."

"An' what in the worl' is a-goin' to become of us, an' that cow got to runnin' away so, I'm afeared all the time she'll git in the mash?" Her tone was querulous, but it was not positive, and when her husband said again, "I'm a-gwine," she said no more, and all the time she was getting together the few things which Cove would take.

As for Vashti, she seemed suddenly revivified; she moved about with a new step, swift, supple, silent, her head up, a new light in her face, and her eyes, as they turned now and then on her father, filled with a new fire. She did not talk much. "I'll a-teck care o' us all," she said once; and once again, when her mother gave something like a moan, she supported her with a word about "the only ones as gives three from one family." It was a word in season, for the mother caught the spirit, and a moment later declared, with a new tone in her voice, that that was better than Mrs. Stanley, and still they were better off than she, for they still had two left to help each other, while she had not a soul.

"I'll teck care o' us all," repeated the girl once more.

It was only a few things that Cove Mills took with him that morning, when he set out in the darkness to overtake the company before they should break camp—hardly his old game-bag half full; for the equipment of the boys had stripped the little cabin of everything that could be of use. He might only have seemed to be going hunting, as he slung down the path with his old long-barrelled gun in his hand and his game-bag over his shoulder, and disappeared in the darkness from the eyes of the two women standing in the cabin door.

The next morning Mrs. Mills paid Mrs. Stanley the first visit she had paid on that side the branch since the day, three years before, when Cove and the boys had the row with Little Darby. It might have seemed accidental, but Mrs. Stanley was the first person in the district to know that all the Mills men were gone to the army. She went over again, from time to time, for it was not a period to keep up open hostilities, and she was younger than Mrs. Stanley and better off; but Vashti never went, and Mrs. Stanley never asked after her or came.

II

THE company in which Little Darby and the Millses had enlisted was one of the many hundred infantry companies which joined and were merged in the Confederate army. It was in no way particularly signalized by anything that it did. It was commanded by the gentleman who did most toward getting it up; and the officers were gentlemen. The seventy odd men who made the rank and file were of all classes, from the sons of the oldest and wealthiest planters in the neighborhood to Little Darby and the dwellers in the district. The war was very different from what those who went into it expected it to be. Until it had gone on some time it seemed mainly marching and camping and staying in camp, quite uselessly as seemed to many, and drilling and doing nothing. Much of the time—especially later on—was given to marching and getting food; but drilling and camp duties at first took up most of it. This was especially hard on the poorer men, no one knew what it was to them.

Little Darby

Some moped, some fell sick. Of the former class was Little Darby. He was too strong to be sickly as one of the Mills boys was, who died of fever in hospital only three months after they went in, and too silent to be as the other, who was jolly and could dance and sing a good song and was soon very popular in the company; more popular even than Old Cove, who was popular in several rights, as being about the oldest man in the company and as having a sort of dry wit when he was in a good humor, which he generally was. Little Darby was hardly distinguished at all, unless by the fact that he was somewhat taller than most of his comrades and somewhat more taciturn. He was only a common soldier of a common class in an ordinary infantry company, such a company as was common in the army. He still had the little wallet which he had picked up in the path that morning he left home. He had asked both of the Mills boys vaguely if they ever had owned such a piece of property, but they had not, and when old Cove told him that he had not either, he had contented himself and carried it about with him somewhat elaborately wrapped up and tied in an old piece of oilcloth and in his inside jacket pocket for safety, with a vague feeling that some day he might find the owner or return it. He was never on specially good terms with the Millses. Indeed, there was always a trace of coolness between them and him. He could not give it to them. Now and then he untied and unwrapped it in a secret place and read a little in the Testament, but that was all. He never touched a needle or so much as a pin, and when he untied the parcel he generally counted them to see that they were all there.

So the war went on, with battles coming a little oftener and food growing ever a little scarcer; but the company was about as before, nothing particular—what with killing and fever a little thinned, a good deal faded; and Little Darby just one in a crowd, marching with the rest, sleeping with the rest, fighting with the rest, starving with the rest. He was hardly known for a long time, except for his silence, outside of his mess. Men were fighting and getting killed or wounded constantly; as for him, he was never touched; and as he did what he was ordered silently and was silent when he got through, there was no one to sing his praise. Even when he was sent out on the skirmish line as a sharp-shooter, if he did anything no one knew it. He would disappear over a crest, or in a wood, and reappear as silent as if he were hunting in the swamps of the district;

clean his gun; cut up wood; eat what he could get, and sit by the fire and listen to the talk, as silent awake as asleep.

One other thing distinguished him, he could handle an axe better than any man in the company; but no one thought much of that—least of all, Little Darby; it only brought him a little more work occasionally.

One day, in the heat of a battle which the men knew was being won, if shooting and cheering and rapid advancing could tell anything, the advance which had been going on with spirit was suddenly checked by a murderous artillery fire which swept the top of a slope, along the crest of which ran a road a little raised between two deep ditches topped by the remains of heavy fences. The infantry, after a gallant and hopeless charge, were ordered to lie down in the ditch behind the pike, and were sheltered from the leaden sleet which swept the crest. Artillery was needed to clear the field beyond, by silencing the batteries which swept it, but no artillery could get into position for the ditches, and the day seemed about to be lost. The only way was up the pike, and the only break was a gate opening into the field right on top of the hill. The gate was gone, but two huge wooden gate-posts, each a tree-trunk, still stood and barred the way. No cannon had room to turn in between them; a battery had tried and a pile of dead men, horses, and debris marked its failure. A general officer galloped up with two or three of his staff to try to start the advance again. He saw the impossibility.

"If we could get a couple of batteries into that field for three minutes," he said, "it would do the work, but in ten minutes it will be too late."

The company from the old county was lying behind the bank almost exactly opposite the gate, and every word could be heard.

Where the axe came from no one knew; but a minute later a man slung himself across the road, and the next second the sharp, steady blows of an axe were ringing on the pike. The axeman had cut a wide cleft in the brown wood, and the big chips were flying before his act was quite taken in, and then a cheer went up from the line. It was no time to cheer, however; other chips were flying than those from the cutter's axe, and the bullets hissed by him like bees, splintering the hard post and knocking the dust from the road about his feet; but he took no notice of them, his axe plied as steadily as if he had been cutting a tree in the woods of the district, and when he had cut one side, he turned as deliberately and cut the other; then placing his hand high up, he flung his weight against the post and it went down. A great cheer went up and the axeman swung back across the road just as two batteries of artillery tore through the opening he had made.

Few men outside of his company knew who the man was, and few had time to ask; for the battle was on again and the infantry pushed forward. As for Little Darby himself, the only thing he said was, "I knowed I could cut it down in ten minutes." He had nine bullet holes through his clothes that night, but Little Darby thought nothing of it, and neither did others; many others had bullet holes through their bodies that night. It happened not long afterward that the general was talking of the battle to an English gentleman who had come over to see something of the war and was visiting him in his camp, and he mentioned the incident of a battle won by an axeman's coolness, but did not know the name of the man who cut the post away; the captain of the company, however, was the general's cousin and was dining with his guest that day, and he said with pride that he knew the man, that he was in his company, and he gave the name.

"It is a fine old name," said the visitor.

"And he is a fine man," said the captain; but none of this was ever known by Darby. He was not mentioned in the gazette, because there was no gazette. The confederate soldiery had no honors save the approval of their own consciences and the love of their own people. It was not even mentioned in the district; or, if it was, it was only that he had cut down a post; other men were being shot to pieces all the time and the district had other things to think of.

Poor at all times, the people of the district were now absolutely without means of subsistence. Fortunately for them, they were inured to hardship; and their men being all gone to the war, the women made such shift as they could and lived as they might. They hoed their little patches, fished the streams, and trapped in the woods. But it was poor enough at best, and the weak went down and only the strong survived. Mrs. Mills was better off than most, she had a cow—at first, and she had Vashti. Vashti turned out to be a tower of strength. She trapped more game than anyone in the district; caught more fish with lines and traps—she went miles to fish below the forks where the fish were bigger than above; she learned to shoot with her father's old gun, which had been sent back when he got a musket, shot like a man and better than most men; she hoed the patch, she tended the cow till it was lost, and then she did many other things. Her mother declared that, when Chris died (Chris was the boy who died of fever), but for Vashti she could not have got along at all, and there were many other women in the pines who felt the same thing.

When the news came that Bob Askew was killed, Vashti was one of the first who got to Bob's wife; and when Billy Luck disappeared in a battle, Vashti gave the best reasons for thinking he had been taken prisoner; and many a string of fish and many a squirrel and hare found their way into the empty cabins because Vashti "happened to pass by."

From having been rather stigmatized as "that Vashti Mills," she came to be relied on, and "Vashti" was consulted and quoted as an authority.

One cabin alone she never visited. The house of old Mrs. Stanley, now almost completely buried under its unpruned wistaria vine, she never entered. Her mother, as has been said, sometimes went across the bottom, and now and then took with her a hare or a bird or a string of fish—on condition from Vashti that it should not be known she had caught them ; but Vashti never went, and Mrs. Mills found herself sometimes put to it to explain to others her unneighborliness. The best she could make of it to say that "Vashti, she always *do* do her own way."

How Mrs. Stanley's wood-pile was kept up nobody knew, if, indeed, it could be called a woodpile, when it was only a recurring supply of dry-wood thrown as if accidentally just at the edge of the clearing. Mrs. Stanley was not of an imaginative turn, even of enough to explain how it came that so much dry-wood came to be there broken up just the right length ; and Mrs. Mills knew no more than that "that cow was always a-goin' off and a-keepin' Vashti a-huntin' everywheres in the worl'."

All said, however, the women of the district had a hungry time, and the war bore on them heavily as on everyone else, and as it went on they suffered more and more. Many a woman went day after day and week after week without even the small portion of coarse corn-bread which was ordinarily her common fare. They called oftener and oftener at the house of their neighbors who owned the plantations near them, and always received something; but as time went on the plantations themselves were stripped; the little things they could take with them when they went, such as eggs, honey, etc., were wanting, and to go too often without anything to give might make them seem like beggars, and that they were not. Their husbands and sons were in the army fighting for the South, as well as those from the plantations, and they stood by this fact on the same level.

The arrogant looks of the negroes were unpleasant, and in marked contrast to the universal graciousness of their owners, but they were slaves and they could afford to despise them. Only they must uphold their independence. Thus no one outside knew what the women of the district went through. When they wrote to their husbands or sons that they were in straits, it meant that they were starving. Such a letter meant all the more because they were used to hunger, but not to writing, and a letter meant perhaps days of thought and enterprise and hours of labor.

As the war went on the hardships everywhere grew heavier and heavier; the letters from home came oftener and oftener. Many of the men got furloughs when they were in winter quarters, and sometimes in summer, too, from wounds, and went home to see their families. Little Darby never went; he sent his mother his pay, and wrote to her, but he did not even apply for a furlough, and he had never been touched except for a couple of flesh wounds which were barely skin-deep. When he heard from his mother she was always cheerful; and as he knew Vashti had never even visited her, there was no other reason for his going home. It was in the late part of the third campaign of the war that he began to think of going.

When Cove Mills got a letter from his wife and told Little Darby how "ailin'" and "puny" his mother was getting, Darby knew that the letter was written by Vashti, and he felt that it meant a great deal. He applied for a furlough, but was told that no furloughs would be granted then—which then meant that work was expected. It came shortly afterward, and Little Darby and the company were in it. Battle followed battle. A good many men in the company were killed, but, as it happened, not one of the men from the district was among them, until one day when the company after a fierce charge found itself hugging the ground in a wide field, on the far side of which the enemy — infantry and artillery —was posted in force. Lying down they were pretty well protected by the conformation of the ground from the artillery; and lying down, the infantry generally, even with their better guns, could not hurt them to a great extent; but a line of sharp-shooters, well placed behind cover of scattered rocks on the far side of the field, could reach them with their long-range rifles, and galled them with their dropping fire, picking off man after man. A line of sharp-shooters was thrown forward to drive them in; but their guns were not as good and the cover was inferior, and it was only after numerous losses that they succeeded in silencing most of them. They still left several men up among the rocks, who from time to time sent a bullet into the line with deadly effect. One man, in particular, ensconced behind a rock on the hill-side, picked off the men with unerring accuracy. Shot after shot was sent at him. At last he was quiet for so long that it seemed he must have been silenced, and they began to hope; Ad Mills rose to his knees and in sheer bravado waved his hat in triumph. Just as he did so a puff of white came from the rock, and Ad Mills threw up his hands and fell on his back, like a log, stone dead. A groan of mingled rage and dismay went along the line. Poor old Cove crept over and fell on the boy's body with a flesh wound in his own arm. Fifty shots were sent at the rock, but a puff of smoke from it afterward and a hissing bullet showed that the marksman was untouched. It was apparent that he was secure behind his rock bulwark and had some opening through which he could fire at his leisure. It was also apparent that he must be dislodged if possible; but how to do it was the question; no one could reach him. The slope down and the slope up to the group of rocks behind which he lay were both in plain view, and any man would be riddled who attempted to cross it. A bit of woods reached some distance up on one side, but not far enough to give a shot at one behind the rock; and though the ground in that direction dipped a little, there was one little ridge in full view of both lines and perfectly bare, except for a number of bodies of skirmishers who had fallen earlier in the day. It was discussed in the line; but everyone knew that no man could get across the ridge alive. While they were talking of it Little Darby, who, with a white face, had helped old Cove to get his boy's body back out of fire, slipped off to one side, rifle in hand, and disappeared in the wood.

They were still talking of the impossibility of dislodging the sharp-shooter when a man appeared on the edge of the wood. He moved swiftly across the sheltered ground, stooping

Little Darby

low until he reached the edge of the exposed place, where he straightened up and made a dash across it. He was recognized instantly by some of the men of his company as Little Darby, and a buzz of astonishment went along the line. What could he mean, it was sheer madness; the line of white smoke along the wood and the puffs of dust about his feet showed that bullets were raining around him. The next second he stopped dead-still, threw up his arms, and fell prone on his face in full view of both lines. A groan went up from his comrades; the whole company knew he was dead, and on the instant a puff of white from the rock and a hissing bullet told that the sharpshooter there was still intrenched in his covert. The men were discussing Little Darby, when someone cried out and pointed to him. He was still alive, and not only alive, but was moving—moving slowly but steadily up the ridge and nearer on a line with the sharpshooter, as flat on the ground as any of the motionless bodies about him. A strange thrill of excitement went through the company as the dark object dragged itself nearer to the rock, and it was not allayed when the whack of a bullet and the well-known white puff of smoke recalled them to the sharp-shoot-

Little Darby

er's dangerous aim; for the next second the creeping figure sprang erect and made a dash for the spot. He had almost reached it when the sharp-shooter discovered him, and the men knew that Little Darby had underestimated the quickness of his hand and aim; for at the same moment the figure of the man behind the rock appeared for a second as he sprang erect; there was a puff of white and Little Darby stopped and staggered and sank to his knees. The next second, however, there was a puff from where he knelt, and then he sank flat once more, and a moment later rolled over on his face on the near side of the rock and just at its foot. There were no more bullets sent from that rock that day—at least, against the Confederates—and that night Little Darby walked into his company's bivouac, dusty from head to foot and with a bullet-hole in his clothes not far from his heart; but he said it was only a spent bullet and had just knocked the breath out of him. He was pretty sore from it for a time, but was able to help old Cove to get his boy's body off and to see him start; for the old man's wound, though not dangerous, was enough to disable him and get him a furlough, and he determined to take his son's body home, which the captain's influence enabled him to do. Between his wound and his grief the old man was nearly helpless, and accepted Darby's silent assistance with mute gratitude. Darby asked him to tell his mother that he was getting on well, and sent her what money he had—his last two months' pay—not enough to have bought her a pair of stockings or a pound of sugar. The only other message he sent was given at the station just as Cove set out. He said:

"Tell Vashti as I got him as done it."

Old Cove grasped his hand tremulously and faltered his promise to do so, and the next moment the train crawled away and left Darby to plod back to camp in the rain, vague and lonely in the remnant of what had once been a gray uniform. If there was one thing that troubled him it was that he could not return Vashti the needle-case until he replaced the broken needles—and there were so many of them broken.

After this Darby was in some sort known, and was put pretty constantly on sharp-shooter service.

The men went into winter quarters before Darby heard anything from home. It came one day in the shape of a letter in the only hand in the world he knew—Vashti's. What it could mean he could not divine—was his mother dead? This was the principal thing that occurred to him. He studied the outside. It had been on the way a month by the postmark, for letters travelled slowly in those days, and a private soldier in an infantry company was hard to find unless the address was pretty clear, which this was not. He did not open it immediately. His mother must be dead, and this he could not face. Nothing else would have made Vashti write. At last he went off alone and opened it, and read it, spelling it out with some pains. It began without an address, with the simple statement that her father had arrived with Ad's body and that it had been buried, and that his wound was right bad and her mother was mightily cut up with her trouble. Then it mentioned his mother and said she had come to Ad's funeral, though she could not walk much now and had never been over to their side since the day after he—Darby—had enlisted; but her father had told her as how he had killed the man as shot Ad, and so she made out to come that far. Then the letter broke off from giving news, and as if under stress of feelings long pent up, suddenly broke loose: she declared that she loved him; that she had always loved him—always—ever since he had been so good to her—a great big boy to a little bit of a girl—at school, and that she did not know why she had been so mean to him; for when she had treated him worst she had loved him most; that she had gone down the path that night when they had met, for the purpose of meeting him and of letting him know she loved him; but something had made her treat him as she did, and all the time she could have let him kill her for love of him. She said she had told her mother and father she loved him and she had tried to tell his mother, but she could not, for she was afraid of her; but she wanted him to tell her when he came; and she had tried to help her and keep her in wood ever since he went away, for his sake. Then the letter told how poorly his mother was and how she had failed of late, and she said she thought he ought to get a furlough and come home, and when he did she would marry him. It was not very well written, nor wholly coherent; at least it took some time to sink fully into Darby's somewhat dazed intellect; but in time he took it in, and when he did he sat like a man overwhelmed. At the end of the letter, as if possibly she thought, in the greatness of her relief at her confession, that the temptation she held out might prove too great even for him, or possibly only because she was a woman.

there was a postscript scrawled across the coarse, blue Confederate paper: "Don't come without a furlough; for if you don't come honorable I won't marry you." This, however, Darby scarcely read. His being was in the letter. It was only later that the picture of his mother ill and failing came to him, and it smote him in the midst of his happiness and clung to him afterward like a nightmare. It haunted him. She was dying.

He applied for a furlough; but furloughs were hard to get then and he could not hear from it; and when a letter came in his mother's name in a lady's hand which he did not know, telling him of his mother's poverty and sickness and asking him if he could get off to come and see her, it seemed to him that she was dying, and he did not wait for the furlough. He was only a few days' march from home and he felt that he could see her and get back before he was wanted. So one day he set out in the rain. It was a scene of desolation that he passed through, for the country was the seat of war; fences were gone, woods burnt, and fields cut up and bare; and it rained all the time. A little before morning, on the night of the third day, he reached the edge of the district and plunged into its well-known pines, and just as day broke he entered the old path which led up the little hill to his mother's cabin. All during his journey he had been picturing the meeting with some one else besides his mother, and if Vashti had stood before him as he crossed the old log he would hardly have been surprised. Now, however, he had other thoughts; as he reached the old clearing he was surprised to find it grown up in small pines already almost as high as his head, and tall weeds filled the rows among the old peach-trees and grew up to the very door. He had been struck by the desolation all the way as he came along; but it had not occurred to him that there must be a change at his own home; he had always pictured it as he left it, as he had always thought of Vashti in her pink calico, with her hat in her hand and her heavy hair almost falling down over her neck. Now a great horror seized him. The door was wet and black. His mother must be dead. He stopped and peered through the darkness at the dim little structure. There was a little smoke coming out of the chimney, and the next instant he strode up to the door. It was shut, but the string was hanging out and he pulled it and pushed the door open. A thin figure seated in the small split-bottomed chair on the hearth, hovering as close as possible over the fire, straightened up and turned slowly as he stepped into the room, and he recognized his mother—but how changed! She was quite white and little more than a skeleton. At sight of the figure behind her she pulled herself to her feet, and peered at him through the gloom.

"Mother!" he said.

"Darby!" She reached her arms toward him, but tottered so that she would have fallen, had he not caught her and eased her down into her chair.

As she became a little stronger she made him tell her about the battles he was in. Mr. Mills had come to tell her that he had killed the man who killed Ad. Darby was not a good narrator, however, and what he had to tell was told in a few words. The old woman revived under it, however, and her eyes had a brighter light in them.

Darby was too much engrossed in taking care of his mother that day to have any thought of any one else. He was used to a soldier's scant fare, but had never quite taken in the fact that his mother and the women at home had less even than they in the field. He had never seen, even in their poorest days after his father's death, not only the house absolutely empty, but without any means of getting anything outside. It gave him a thrill to think what she must have endured without letting him know. As soon as he could leave her, he went into the woods with his old gun, and shortly returned with a few squirrels which he cooked for her; the first meat, she told him, that she had tasted for weeks. On hearing it his heart grew hot. Why had not Vashti come and seen about her? She explained it partly, however, when she told him that every one had been sick at Cove Mills's, and old Cove himself had come near dying. No doctor could be got to see them, as there was none left in the neighborhood, and but for Mrs. Douwill she did not know what they would have done. But Mrs. Douwill was down herself now.

The young man wanted to know about Vashti, but all he could manage to make his tongue ask was,

"Vashti?"

She could not tell him, she did not know anything about Vashti. Mrs. Mills used to bring her things sometimes, till she was taken down, but Vashti had never come to see her; all she knew was that she had been sick with the others.

That she had been sick awoke in the young man a new tenderness, the deeper because he had done her an injustice; and he was seized with a great longing to see her. All his old love seemed suddenly accumulated in his heart, and he determined to go and see her at once, as he had not long to stay. He set about his little preparations forthwith, putting on his old clothes which his mother had kept ever since he went away, as being more presentable than the old worn and muddy, threadbare uniform, and brushing his long yellow hair and beard into something like order. He changed from one coat to the other the little package which he always carried, thinking that he would show it to her with the hole in it, which the sharp-shooter's bullet had made that day, and he put her letter into the same pocket; his heart beating at the sight of her hand and the memory of the words she had written, and then he set out. It was already late in the evening, and after the rain the air was soft and balmy, though the western sky was becoming overcast again by a cloud, which low down on the horizon was piling up mountain on mountain of vapor, as if it might rain again by night. Darby, however, having dressed, crossed the flat without much trouble, only getting a little wet in some places where the logs were gone. As he turned into the path up the hill, he stood face to face with Vashti. She was standing by a little spring which came from under an old oak, the only one on the hill-side of pines, and was in a faded black calico. He scarcely took in at first that it was Vashti, she was so changed. He had always thought of her as he last saw her that evening in pink, with her white throat and her scornful eyes. She was older now than she was then; looked more a woman and taller; and her throat if anything was whiter than ever against her black dress; her face was whiter too, and her eyes darker and larger. At least, they opened wide when Darby appeared in the path. Her hands went up to her throat as if she suddenly wanted breath. All of the young man's heart went out to her, and the next moment he was within arm's length of her. Her one word was in his ears:

"Darby!" He was about to catch her in his arms when a gesture restrained him, and her look turned him to stone.

"Yer uniform?" she gasped, stepping back. Darby was not quick always, and he looked down at his clothes and then at her again, his dazed brain wondering.

"Whar's yer uniform?" she asked.

"At home," he said, quietly, still wondering. She seemed to catch some hope.

"Yer got a furlough?" she said, more quietly, coming a little nearer to him, and her eyes growing softer.

"Got a furlough?" he repeated to gain time for thought. "I—I——" He had never thought of it before; the words in her letter flashed into his mind, and he felt his face flush. He would not tell her a lie. "No, I ain't got no furlough," he said, and paused whilst he tried to get his words together to explain. But she did not give him time.

"What you doin' with them clo'se on?" she asked again.

"I—I——" he began, stammering as her suspicion dawned on him.

"You're a deserter!" she said, coldly, leaning forward, her hands clenched, her face white, her eyes contracted.

"A what!" he asked aghast, his brain not wholly taking in her words.

"You're a deserter!" she said again—"and —a coward!"

All the blood in him seemed to surge to his head and leave his heart like ice. He seized her arm with a grip like steel.

"Vashti Mills," he said, with his face white, "don't you say that to me—if yer were a man I'd kill yer right here where yer stan'!" He tossed her hand from him, and turned on his heel.

The next instant she was standing alone, and when she reached the point in the path where she could see the crossing, Darby was already on the other side of the swamp, striding knee-deep through the water as if he were on dry land. She could not have made him hear if she had wished it; for on a sudden a great rushing wind swept through the pines, bending them down like grass and blowing the water in the bottom into white waves, and the thunder which had been rumbling in the distance suddenly broke with a great peal just overhead.

In a few minutes the rain came; but the girl did not mind it. She stood looking across the bottom until it came in sheets, wetting her to the skin and shutting out everything a few yards away.

The thunder-storm passed, but all that night the rain came down, and all the next day, and when it held up a little in the evening the bottom was a sea.

The rain had not prevented Darby from going out—he was used to it; and he spent most of the day away from home. When he returned he brought his mother a few provisions, as much meal perhaps as a child might carry, and spent the rest of the evening sitting before the fire, silent and motionless, a flame burning back deep in his eyes and a cloud fixed on his brow. He was in his uniform, which he had put on again the night before as soon as he got home, and the steam rose from it as he sat. The other clothes were in a bundle on the floor where he had tossed them the evening before. He never moved except when his mother now and then spoke, and then sat down again as before. Presently he rose and said he must be going; but as he rose to his feet, a pain shot through him like a knife; everything turned black before him and he staggered and fell full length on the floor.

He was still on the floor next morning, for his mother had not been able to get him to the bed, or to leave to get any help; but she had made him a pallet, and he was as comfortable as a man might be with a raging fever. Feeble as she was, the sudden demand on her had awakened the old woman's faculties and she was stronger than might have seemed possible. One thing puzzled her: in his incoherent mutterings, Darby constantly referred to a furlough and a deserter. She knew that he had a furlough, of course; but it puzzled her to hear him constantly repeating the words. So the day passed and then, Darby's delirium still continuing, she made out to get to a neighbor's to ask help. The neighbor had to go to Mrs. Douwill's as the only place where there was a chance of getting any medicine, and it happened that on the way back she fell in with a couple of soldiers, on horseback, who asked her a few questions. They were members of a home and conscript guard just formed, and when she left them they had learned her errand.

Fortunately, Darby's illness took a better turn next day, and by sunset he was free from delirium.

Things had not fared well over at Cove Mills's during these days any more than at Mrs. Stanley's. Vashti was in a state of mind which made her mother wonder if she were not going crazy. She set it down to the storm she had been out in that evening, for Vashti had not mentioned Darby's name. She kept his pressence to herself, thinking that—thinking so many things that she could not speak or eat. Her heart was like lead within her; but she could not rid herself of the thought of Darby. She could have torn it out for hate of herself; and to all her mother's questioning glances she turned the face of a sphinx. For two days she neither ate nor spoke. She watched the opposite hill through the rain which still kept up —something was going on over there, but what it was she could not tell. At last, on the evening of the third day, she could stand it no longer, and she set out from home to learn something; she could not have gone to Mrs. Stanley's, even if she had wished to do so; for the bottom was still a sea extending from side to side, and it was over her head in the current. She set off, therefore, up the stream on her own side, thinking to learn something up that way. She met the woman who had taken the medicine to Darby that evening, and she told her all she knew, mentioning among other things the men of the conscript guard she had seen. Vashti's heart gave a sudden bound up into her throat. As she was so near she went on up to the Cross-roads; but just as she stepped out into the road before she reached there, she came on a small squad of horsemen riding slowly along. She stood aside to let them pass; but they drew in and began to question her as to the roads about them. They were in long cloaks and overcoats, and she thought they were the conscript guard, especially as there was a negro with them who seemed to know the roads and to be showing them the way. Her

Little Darby

one thought was of Darby; he would be arrested and shot. When they questioned her, therefore, she told them of the roads leading to the big river around the fork and quite away from the district. Whilst they were still talking, more riders came around the curve, and the next instant Vashti was in the midst of a column of cavalry, and she knew that they were the Federals. She had one moment of terror for herself as the restive horses trampled around her, and the calls and noises of a body of cavalry moving dinned in her ears; but the next moment, when the others gave way and a man whom she knew to be the commander pressed forward and began to question her, she forgot her own terror in fear for her cause. She had all her wits about her instantly; and under a pretence of repeating what she had already told the first men, she gave them such a mixture of descriptions that the negro was called up to unravel it. She made out that they were trying to reach the big river by a certain road, and marched in the night as well as in the day. She admitted that she had never been on that road but once. And when she was taken along with them a mile or two to the place where they went into bivouac until the moon should rise, she soon gave such an impression of her denseness and ignorance that, after a little more questioning, she was told that she might go home if she could find her way, and was sent by the commander out of the camp. She was no sooner out of hearing of her captors than she began to run with all her speed. Her chief thought was of Darby. Deserter as he was, and dead to her, he was a man, and could advise her, help her. She tore through the woods the nearest way, unheeding the branches which caught and tore her clothes; the stream, even where she struck it, was out of its banks; but she did not heed it—she waded through, it reaching about to her waist, and struck out again at the top of her speed.

It must have been a little before midnight when she emerged from the pines in front of the Stanley cabin. The latch-string was out, and she knocked and pushed open the door almost simultaneously. All she could make out to say was, "Darby." The old woman was on her feet, and the young man was sitting up in the bed, by the time she entered.

Darby was the first to speak.

"What do you want here?" he asked, sternly.

"Darby—the Yankees—all around," she gasped—"out on the road yonder."

Little Darby

"What!"

A minute later the young man, white as a ghost, was getting on his jacket while she told her story, beginning with what the woman she had met had told her of the two men she had seen. The presence of a soldier had given her confidence, and having delivered her message both women left everything else to him. His experience or his soldier's instinct told him what they were doing and also how to act. They were a raid which had gotten around the body of the army and were striking for the capital; and from their position, unless they could be delayed they might surprise it. In the face of the emergency a sudden genius seemed to illuminate the young man's mind. By the time he was dressed he was ready with his plan —Did Vashti know where any of the conscript guard stayed?

Yes, down the road at a certain place. Good; it was on the way. Then he gave her his orders. She was to go to this place and rouse any one she might find there and tell them to send a messenger to the city with all speed to warn them, and were to be themselves if possible at a certain point on the road by which the raiders were travelling, where a little stream crossed it in a low place in a heavy piece of swampy woods. They would find a barricade there and a small force might possibly keep them back. Then she was to go on down and have the bridge, ten or twelve miles below on the road between the forks burned, and if necessary was to burn it herself; and it must be done by sunrise. But they were on the other road, outside of the forks, the girl explained, to which Darby only said, he knew that, but they would come back and try the bridge road.

"And you burn the bridge if you have to do it with your own hand, you hear—and now go," he said.

"Yes—I'll do it," said the girl obediently and turned to the door. The next instant she turned back to him: he had his gun and was getting his axe.

"And, Darby——?" she began falteringly, her heart in her eyes.

"Go," said the young soldier, pointing to the door, and she went just as he took up his old rifle and stepped over to where his mother sat white and dumb. As she turned at the edge of the clearing and looked back up the path over the pine-bushes she saw him step out of the door with his gun in one hand and his axe in the other.

An hour later Darby, with the fever still hot

Little Darby

on him, was cutting down trees in the darkness on the bank of a marshy little stream, and throwing them into the water on top of one another across the road, in a way to block it beyond a dozen axemen's work for several hours, and Vashti was trudging through the darkness miles away to give the warning. Every now and then the axeman stopped cutting and listened, and then went on again. He had cut down a half-dozen trees and formed a barricade which it would take hours to clear away before cavalry could pass, when, stopping to listen, he heard a sound that caused him to put down his axe: the sound of horses splashing along through the mud. His practised ear told him that there were only three or four of them, and he took up his gun and climbed up on the barricade and waited. Presently the little squad of horsemen came in sight, a mere black group in the road. They saw the dark mass lying across the road and reined in; then after a colloquy came on down slowly. Darby waited until they were within fifty yards of his barricade, and then fired at the nearest one. A horse wheeled, plunged, and then galloped away in the darkness, and several rounds from pistols were fired toward him, whilst something went on on the ground. Before he could finish reloading, however, the men had turned around and were out of sight. In a minute Darby climbed over the barricade and strode up the road after them. He paused where the man he had shot had fallen. The place in the mud was plain; but his comrades had taken him up and carried him off. Darby hurried along after them. Day was just breaking, and the body of cavalry were preparing to leave their bivouac when a man emerged from the darkness on the opposite side of the camp from that where Little Darby had been felling trees, and walked up to the picket. He was halted and brought up where the fire-light could shine on him, and was roughly questioned —a tall young countryman, very pale and thin, with an old ragged slouched hat pulled over his eyes, and an old patched uniform on his gaunt frame. He did not seem at all disturbed by the pistols displayed around him, but seated himself at the fire and looked about in a dull kind of way.

"What do you want?" they asked him, seeing how cool he was.

"Don't you want a guide?" he asked, drawlingly.

"Who are you?" inquired the corporal in charge. He paused.

"Some calls me a d'serter," he said, slowly.

The men all looked at him curiously.

"Well, what do you want?"

"I thought maybe as you wanted a guide," he said, quietly.

"We don't want you. We've got all the guide we want," answered the corporal, roughly, "and we don't want any spies around here either, you understand?"

"Does he know the way? All the creeks is up now, an' it's sort o' hard to git erlong through down yonder way if you don't know the way toller'ble well?"

"Yes, he knows the way too—every foot of it—and a good deal more than you'll see of it if you don't look out."

"Oh! That road down that way is sort o' stopped up," said the man, as if he were carrying on a connected narrative and had not heard him. "They's soldiers on it too a little fur'er down, and they's done got word you're a-comin' that a-way."

"What's that?" they asked, sharply.

"Leastways it's stopped up, and I knows a way down this a-way in and about as nigh as that," went on the speaker, in the same level voice.

"Where do you live?" they asked him.

"I lives back in the pines here a piece."

"How long have you lived here?"

"About twenty-three years, I b'leeves; 'ats what my mother says."

"You know all the country about here?"

"Ought to."

"Been in the army?"

"Ahn—hahn."

"What did you desert for?"

Darby looked at him leisurely.

"'D you ever know a man as 'lowed he'd deserted? I never did." A faint smile flickered on his pale face.

He was taken to the camp before the commander, a dark, self-contained looking man with a piercing eye and a close mouth, and there closely questioned as to the roads, and he gave the same account he had already given. The negro guide was brought up and his information tallied with the new comer's as far as he knew it, though he knew well only the road which they were on and which Darby said was stopped up. He knew, too, that a road such as Darby offered to take them by ran somewhere down that way and joined the road they were on a good distance below; but he thought it was a good deal longer way and they had to cross a fork of the river.

There was a short consultation between the

commander and one or two other officers, and then the commander turned to Darby, and said:

"What you say about the road's being obstructed this way is partly true; do you guarantee that the other road is clear?"

Darby paused and reflected.

"I'll guide you," he said, slowly.

"Do you guarantee that the bridge on the river is standing and that we can get across?"

"Hit's standing now, fur as I know."

"Do you understand that you are taking your life in your hand?"

Darby looked at him coolly.

"And that if you take us that way and for any cause—for any cause whatsoever we fail to get through safe, we will hang you to the nearest tree?"

Darby waited as if in deep reflection.

"I understand," he said. "I'll guide you."

The silence that followed seemed to extend all over the camp. The commander was reflecting and the others had their eyes fastened on Darby. As for him, he sat as unmoved as if he had been alone in the woods.

"All right," said the leader, suddenly, "it's a bargain: we'll take your road. What do you want?"

Little Darby

"Could you gi'me a cup o' coffee? It's been some little time since I had anything to eat, an' I been sort o' sick."

"You shall have 'em," said the officer, "and good pay besides, if you lead us straight; if not, a limb and a halter rein; you understand?"

A quarter of an hour later they were on the march, Darby trudging in front down the middle of the muddy road between two of the advance guard, whose carbines were conveniently carried to insure his fidelity. What he thought of, who might know?—plain; poor; ignorant; unknown; marching every step voluntarily nearer to certain and ignominious death for the sake of his cause.

As day broke they saw a few people who lived near the road, and some of them recognized Darby and looked their astonishment to see him guiding them. One or two of the women broke out at him for a traitor and a dog, to which he said nothing; but only looked a little defiant with two red spots burning in his thin cheeks, and trudged on as before; now and then answering a question; but for the most part silent.

He must have thought of his mother, old and by herself in her cabin; but she would not live long; and of Vashti some. She had called him a deserter, as the other women had done. A verse from the Testament she gave him may have come into his mind; he had never quite understood it: "Blessed are ye when men shall revile ye." Was this what it meant? This and another one seemed to come together. It was something about "enduring hardship like a good soldier," he could not remember it exactly. Yes, he could do that. But Vashti had called him a deserter. Maybe now though she would not; and the words in the letter she had written him came to him, and the little package in his old jacket pocket made a warm place there; and he felt a little fresher than before. The sun came up and warmed him as he trudged along, and the country grew flatter and flatter, and the road deeper and deeper. They were passing down into the bottom. On either side of them were white-oak swamps, so that they could not see a hundred yards ahead; but for several miles Darby had been watching for the smoke of the burning bridge, and as they neared the river his heart began to sink. There was one point on the brow of a hill before descending to the bottom, where a sudden bend of the road and curve of the river two or three miles below gave a sight of the bridge. Darby waited for this, and when he reached it and saw the bridge still standing his heart sank like lead. Other eyes saw it too, and a score of glasses were levelled at it, and a cheer went up.

"Why don't you cheer too?" asked an officer. "You have more to make or lose than anyone else."

"We ain't there yit," said Darby.

Once he thought he had seen a little smoke, but it had passed away, and now they were within three miles of the bridge and there was nothing. What if, after all, Vashti had failed and the bridge was still standing! He would really have brought the raiders by the best way and have helped them. His heart at the thought came up into his throat. He stopped and began to look about as if he doubted the road. When the main body came up, however, the commander was in no doubt, and a pistol stuck against his head gave him to understand that no fooling would be stood. So he had to go on.

As to Vashti, she had covered the fifteen miles which lay between the district and the fork-road; and had found and sent a messenger to give warning in the city; but not finding any of the homeguard where she thought they were, she had borrowed some matches and had trudged on herself to execute the rest of Darby's commands.

The branches were high from the backwater of the fork, and she often had to wade up to her waist, but she kept on, and a little after daylight she came to the river. Ordinarily, it was not a large stream; a boy could chuck a stone across it, and there was a ford above the bridge not very deep in dry weather, which people sometimes took to water their horses, or because they preferred to ride through the water to crossing the steep and somewhat rickety old bridge. Now, however, the water was far out in the woods, and long before the girl got in sight of the bridge she was wading up to her knees. When she reached the point where she could see it, her heart for a moment failed her; the whole flat was under water. She remembered Darby's command, however, and her courage came back to her. She knew that it could not be as deep as it looked between her and the bridge, for the messenger had gone before her that way, and a moment later she had gone back and collected a bundle of "drywood," and with a long pole to feel her way she waded carefully in. As it grew deeper and deeper until it reached her breast, she took the matches out and held them in her teeth, holding her bundle above her head. It was hard work to keep her footing this way, however, and once she stepped into a hole and went under to her chin, having a narrow escape from falling into a place which her pole could not fathom; but she recovered herself and at last was on the bridge. When she tried to light a fire, however, her matches would not strike. They as well as the wood had gotten wet when she slipped, and not one would light. She might as well have been at her home in the district. When every match had been tried and tried again on a dry stone, only to leave a white streak of smoking sulphur on it, she sat down and cried. For the first time she felt cold and weary. The rays of the sun fell on her and warmed her a little, and she wiped her eyes on her sleeve and looked up. The sun had just come up over the hill. It gave her courage. She turned and looked the other way from which she had come—nothing but a waste of water and woods. Suddenly, from a point up over the nearer woods a little sparkle caught her eye; there must be a house there, she thought; they might have matches, and she would go back and get some. But there it was again—it moved. There was another—another —and something black moving. She sprang to her feet and strained her eyes. Good God! they were coming! In a second she had turned the other way, rushed across the bridge, and was dashing through the water to her waist. The water was not wide that way. The hill rose almost abruptly on that side, and up it she dashed, and along the road. A faint curl of smoke caught her eye and she made for it through the field.

It was a small cabin, and the woman in it had just gotten her fire well started for the morning, when a girl bare-headed and barefooted, dripping wet to the skin, her damp hair hanging down her back, her face white and her eyes like coals, rushed in almost without knocking and asked for a chunk of fire. The woman had no time to refuse (she told of it afterward when she described the burning of the bridge); for without waiting for answer and before she really took in that it was not a ghost, the girl had seized the biggest chunk on the hearth and was running with it across the field. In fact, the woman rather thought she was an evil spirit; for she saw her seize a whole panel of fence—more rails than she could have carried to save her life, she said, and dashed with them over the hill.

In Vashti's mind, indeed, it was no time to

waste words, she was back on the bridge with the chunk of fire and an armful of rails before the woman recovered from her astonishment, and was down on her knees blowing her chunk to rekindle it. The rails, however, like everything else, were wet and would not light, and she was in despair. At last she got a little blaze started, but it would not burn fast; it simply smoked. She expected the soldiers to come out of the woods every minute, and every second she was looking up to see if they were in sight. What would Darby think? What would happen if she failed? She sprang up to look around: the old rail of the bridge caught her eye; it was rotted, but what remained was heart and would burn like light-wood. She tore a piece of it down and stuck one end in the fire: it caught and sputtered and suddenly flamed up; the next second she was tearing the rail down all along and piling it on the blaze, and as it caught she dashed back through the water and up the hill, and brought another armful of rails. Back and forth she waded several times and piled on rails until she got a stack of them—two stacks, and the bridge floor dried and caught and began to blaze; and when she brought her last armful it was burning all across. She had been so busy bringing wood that she

Little Darby

had forgotten to look across to the other side for some time, and was only reminded of it as she was wading back with her last armful of rails by something buzzing by her ear, and the second after the crack of a half-dozen guns followed from the edge of the wood the other side. She could not see them well for the burden in her arms, but she made out a number of horses dashing into the water on the little flat, and saw some puffs of smoke about their heads. She was bound to put her wood on, however, so she pushed ahead, went up on the bridge through the smoke as far as she could go, and flung her rails on the now devouring fire. A sudden veer of the wind blew the smoke behind her and bent the flames aside, and she could see clear across the fire to the other bank. She saw a great number of men on horses at the edge of the woods, in a sort of mass; and a half-dozen or so in the water riding up to their saddle-skirts half-way to the bridge, and between the first two, wading in water to his waist, Darby. He was bare-headed and he waved his hat to her, and she heard a single cheer. She waved her hand to him, and there was a little puff of smoke and something occurred in the water among the horses. The smoke from the fire suddenly closed around her and shut out everything from her eyes, and when it blew away again one of the horses had thrown his rider in the water. There was a lot of firing both from the edge of the wood and from the horsemen in the water, and Darby had disappeared.

She made her way back to the bank and plunged into a clump of bushes, where she was hidden and watched the raiders. She saw several of them try to ford the river, one got across but swam back, the others were swept down by the current, and the horse of one got out below without his rider. The other she did not see again.

Soon after their comrade had rejoined them, the men on the edge of the wood turned around and disappeared, and a half-hour later she saw the glint of the sun on their arms and accoutrements as they crossed over the top of the hill returning two miles above.

. . . .

This is the story of the frustration of the raid upon which so much hope was built by some in high position at Washington. A day was lost, and warning was given to the Confederate Government, and the bold plan of the commander of the raiding party was defeated.

As to Little Darby, the furlough he had applied for came, but came too late and was returned. For a time some said he was a deserter; but two women knew differently.

A Federal soldier who was taken prisoner gave an account of the raid. He said that a contraband had come from Washington and undertaken to lead them across the country, and that he had brought them around the head of the streams, when one night a rebel deserter came into camp and undertook to show them a better way by a road which ran between the rivers, but crossed lower down by a bridge; that they had told him that, if for any reason they failed to get through by his road they would hang him, a bargain which he had accepted. That he had led them straight, but when they had got to the bridge it had been set on fire and was burning at that moment; that a half-dozen men, of whom he, the narrator, was one, rode in, taking the guide along with them, to see if they could not put the fire out, or, failing that, find the ford; and when they were about half-way across the little flat they saw the person on the bridge in the very act of burning it, and waving his hand in triumph; and the man who was riding abreast of him in front fired his carbine at him. As he did so the deserter wheeled on him, and said, "God d—n you—don't you

Little Darby

know that's a woman," and springing on him like a tiger tore him from his horse; and, before they took in what he was doing, had, before their very eyes, flung both of them into a place where the current was running, and they had disappeared. They had seen the deserter's head once in the stream lower down, and had fired at him, and he thought had hit him, as he went down immediately and they did not see him again.

This is all that was known of Little Darby, except that a year or more afterward, and nearly a year after Mrs. Stanley's death, a package with an old needle-case in it and a stained little Testament with a bullet hole through it, was left at the Cross-roads, with a message that a man who had died at the house of the person who left it as he was trying to make his way back to his command, asked to have that sent to Vashti Mills.

THE END.

www.ingramcontent.com/pod-product-compliance
Lightning Source LLC
Chambersburg PA
CBHW032144230426
43672CB00011B/2446